Pirin Planina

Tragic and Comic Episodes from Captivity

G. Topîrceanu

George Topîrceanu

Pirin Planina
Tragic and Comic Episodes from Captivity

Translated by Diana Livesay
Illustrated by Olga Rogozenco
Introduction by A.K. Brackob

CENTER FOR
Romanian
STUDIES

The Center for Romanian Studies

Las Vegas ◊ Chicago ◊ Palm Beach

Classics of Romanian Literature
Volume III
ISSN 2693-1796

Published in the United States of America by
Histria Books
7181 N. Hualapai Way, Ste. 130-86
Las Vegas, NV 89166 USA
HistriaBooks.com

The Center for Romanian Studies is an independent academic and cultural institute with the mission to promote knowledge of the history, literature, and culture of Romania in the world. The publishing program of the Center is affiliated with Histria Books. Contributions from scholars from around the world are welcome. To support the work of the Center for Romanian Studies, contact us at info@centerforromanianstudies.com

Library of Congress Control Number: 2023931223

ISBN 978-1-59211-149-7 (hardcover)
ISBN 978-1-59211-463-4 (softbound)
ISBN 978-1-59211-263-0 (eBook)

Introduction

When I first began studying Romanian literature, I was, of course, captivated by the greats, such as Mihai Eminescu and Ion Creangă. As my passion for the amazing literature of the country grew, I began to discover more and more incredible writers. Among these was George Topîrceanu. I was quickly captivated by the humor and wit of this poetic genius and determined that one day the writings of this brilliant Iaşi transplant should be made known to an international audience.

George Topîrceanu is among the seminal writers of twentieth-century Romanian literature. Best known for his lyric humor, Topîrceanu's contributions to literature extend beyond his poetry. He was a man of acute wit and keen insight. In addition to poetry, he wrote prose and essays. He was also an outstanding editor, inspiring the literary careers of many of Romania's most important writers of the interwar period – a time when Romanian culture flourished and Iaşi, the poet's adopted home was considered the cultural capital of the country.

Born in Bucharest on March 20, 1886, George Topîrceanu came from a working-class family. His father, Ion, was a skinner, and his mother, Paraschiva, was a carpet weaver. They had moved to Bucharest from the region around Sibiu sometime before the birth of their second child. Young George attended school in the Romanian capital, graduating from St. Sava High School in 1906.

Early in life, George developed a passion for literature. He would later write, "I was in third grade when I discovered that I could write poems. In the beginning, they provided me with an air of innocence, like an inoffensive game, like any other. I had no idea then what a treasure I came across. I didn't know that the literary bug, when it finds favorable terrain, is enough to enter a single time into an organism so as not to escape from it for a whole life... until they build you a statue."

Topîrceanu made his literary debut while still in high school in 1904, publishing a poem in the humor journal *Belgia Orientului*. He published his early poems in local newspapers and magazines. After graduating high school, he enrolled in the University of Bucharest to study law, but having been bitten by the literary bug, Topîrceanu soon moved to the Faculty of Letters. Still, George did not have the drive to finish his academic studies and instead decided to embark on the literary career he so desired.

By 1909, Topîrceanu's poems began appearing in major literary journals of the time, such as *Sămănătorul*, founded by the famous Romanian poets Alexandru Vlahuță and George Coșbuc. *Sămănătorul* was a successor of the Junimea movement of the nineteenth century and was heavily influenced by the great Romanian historian Nicolae Iorga. It promoted populism, traditional values, and neo-Romanticism.

Young George soon attracted the attention of acclaimed literary critic Gabaret Ibrăileanu, a professor at the University of Iași and the editor of one of the most important literary magazines of the time, *Viața românească*. Impressed by his poetry, Ibrăileanu invited Topîrceanu to come to Iași to take a position as an editor. He quickly adapted to the environment in Iași. Throughout the remainder of his life, he would consider himself a Moldavian.

He would later recall, "When I arrived in Iași from the whirlwind of the capital, I found the editorial office of *Viața românească* situated deep in the back of a yard full of rubbish. There was a sign with the words 'Editorial Office' on the door that led to a narrow room, long and dark, with a table almost as long inside. It was a monumental table as big as a platform where the patriarchal administration of Mr. Mihai Pastia was located, and where one could see two registers of subscribers with eternally messed up accounts."

"It was with these people, in an atmosphere of cordiality, esteem, enthusiasm, and Moldavian indolence that *Viața românească*, issue by issue, month after month, was produced," Topîrceanu fondly reminisced. "And its publication was eagerly awaited by thousands of readers in all social strata, its well-to-do subscribers who never paid for their subscriptions, teachers and intellectuals of our country, priests, and above all students, twenty of whom would chip in to buy a single copy and pass it around until it fell to pieces."

In 1912, George married a young schoolteacher, Victoria Iuga. She would be an inspiration for his literary work, but they had a difficult marriage. Topîrceanu drank heavily and was known to have an eye for the ladies. The couple had one son, Gheorghe.

With the outbreak of the Balkan War in 1913, Topîrceanu was drafted into the army and participated in the campaign in southern Dobrogea. He recorded in his journal the difficult retreat of the soldiers and the devastating cholera outbreak they endured. Following the war, he returned to Iaşi and published two volumes of poems in 1916, *Balade vesele şi triste* and *Parodii originale*.

After the outbreak of World War I, Topîrceanu was again drafted when Romania entered the conflict on the side of the Allied powers. He soon found himself on the front lines of the war as the Romanian and Bulgarian armies confronted each other at Turtucaia in September 1916. After a five-day battle, the Romanian army was routed, and the Danubian fortress fell to the Bulgarians. Over 28,000 Romanian soldiers were captured, among them George Topîrceanu.

For the next two years, Topîrceanu remained a captive in Bulgaria. His time as a prisoner of war is the subject of *Pirin Planina: Tragic and Comic Episodes from Captivity*. It is a book that places the writer's wit and insightfulness on full display.

After returning to Iaşi in 1919, he became an editor, along with his longtime friend, the novelist Mihail Sadoveanu, at the literary journal, *Însemnări literare*. The following year, with the reappearance of *Viaţa românească*, he became editor-in-chief. In 1921, he translated William Shakespeare's *A Midsummer Night's Dream* into Romanian. His reputation as a poet grew steadily and, in 1926, he received the National Poetry Prize.

Topîrceanu was a collector of firearms and a hunter. He was also fascinated by new technologies. In 1930, he became the inspector general for theaters in Moldavia. In June 1935, he gave a famous speech at the University of Iaşi entitled, *How I Became a Moldavian*. In it, one can find a perfect example of his wit and satire:

There is a story about an important member of the once 'Junimea' Society who had never spoken in public and who had to deliver a lecture. When he got to the rostrum all he was able to say was, 'honored audience!...' Then, realizing that he could not utter a single word, being so nervous, he picked up his papers and went home.

I don't know if anyone congratulated him.

But I know one thing for certain. If the speaker had spoken for one hour and a half, as speakers usually do, on a subject of great importance, his lecture would have taken him to the place where all lectures go, that is, to the eternal night of forgetfulness, and nobody would have ever thought of it. But under the circumstances, posterity has preserved the lecture in its entirety, without leaving out a single word, for its literary beauty, for its originality, for its antique brevity.[1]

In 1936, in recognition of his lifetime of work for Romanian literature, he became a corresponding member of the Romanian Academy. He also began working on a new journal, *Însemnări ieşene*. With this new journal, he helped to guide the careers of many promising young writers, among them, Magda Isanos.

On May 7, 1937, George Topîrceanu died of liver cancer, probably aggravated by years of heavy drinking. He was buried in Iaşi's most famous cemetery, Eternitatea, where his grave can be visited today. His home in Iaşi has also been preserved as a museum.

Topîrceanu published three volumes of poetry during his lifetime: *Balade vesele şi triste*, *Parodii originale*, and *Migdale amare*. His poetry is known for its subtle humor, biting sarcasm, and its refined lyricism. His unique style left its mark on Romanian poetry and his work is still studied in Romanian schools today. Romanian critic Al. Săndulescu described his poetry as "Evolving from an epigonic sentimentalism at the beginning to a poetry filled with parodic hu-

---

[1] George Topîrceanu, "How I Became A Moldavian," in *Romanian Civilization*, II:2 (Fall-Winter, 1993), pp. 59-70.

mor, self-irony, a slight melancholy. Topîrceanu is a distinct voice in our poetry."[2] He is one of the few representatives of lyric humor in Romanian poetry.
"In his humor, he almost always hides a note of melancholy and sometimes
even tragedy."[3]

Much of his prose writings, also known for their wit and sarcasm, were published as essays and later collected into volumes. His book *Pirin Planina* was
published in 1936, the year before his death. His unfinished novella, *Minunile
Sfântului Sisoe*, was published posthumously.

Topîrceanu tells the story of how *Pirin Planina* came to be in his preface to
his editor in Bucharest, in which he shows that he had become more Moldavian
than most Moldavians.

George Topîrceanu is a truly unique and gifted writer in Romanian literature, and *Pirin Planina* is a welcome addition to the *Classics of Romanian Literature* series initiated by the Center for Romanian Studies. The series is dedi-
cated to making essential works of Romanian literature available to an international audience and to illustrate the connections of Romanian writers to broader
currents in world literature and culture. It is part of the core mission of the Center for Romanian Studies to promote knowledge of Romanian history, literature, and culture in the world.

Finally, I would like to thank Diana Livesay for her excellent translation of
Topîrceanu's remarkable prose, and Olga Rogozenco for her beautiful illustra-
tions that help to bring the story of Pirin Planina to life for readers. It is our
hope that this book will help to bring international attention to this amazing
writer and pay homage to the service he did for Romanian culture.

A.K. Brackob

---

[2] Al. Săndulescu, "George Topîrceanu," in *Scriitori români*, p. 450.

[3] Ibid., p. 451.

In Lieu of a Prologue

Dearest Mr. Ciornei,

After a financial catastrophe suffered last summer on a Sunday at the Băneasa hippodrome, I woke up sitting in a leather armchair in your editorial office.

Even now, I wonder: what was I doing there? Maybe I came to ask you, just like this, when the train to Iaşi departs.

One thing led to another, and I ended up signing a contract, it appears, through which I was bound to turn over for publication the finished manuscript of a book about my war memories from the time of my captivity in Bulgaria. I somehow recall that you also gave me a sum of money as an advance on future royalties for my book. Do you remember that? If you forgot, it's okay. We can all mind our own business and – nothing more need be said about it.

After I took your advance and returned to Iaşi, I sat and thought about it some more.

Should I write it? Should I not write it?...

The past years have seen so much war literature published! Everyone across the globe is convinced in their hearts, just like before 1914, that war is a calamity, a shame on our civilization, etc. Still, humankind doesn't abolish it. It's like war isn't caused by us humans – it's as if it is caused by some beings from another planet against our unanimous will.

So why then should I write, just so I can also show mankind what war is like?

It seems like the great men, the ones who begin the wars, must be bad people with hearts of stone…

I don't think so.

I saw the Kaiser of Germany in Sofia, who is considered the main architect of the World War. He didn't seem to be a bad man at all. I saw him from a hospital window as he passed by in a car on his way from the train station to the palace. He was laughing. On his left was the king of Bulgaria of those times, but I couldn't see him well because, at that exact moment, he pulled a handkerchief from his pocket and blew his nose.

"What a terrible misfortune war is!" exclaimed Napoleon on the battlefield at Eylau, during an evening when he was cold and only ate baked potatoes because his supplies were delayed – proving through this a great sensibility to the suffering of his people. That was proof that he didn't cause the Napoleonic wars in which a million people scattered their bones on so many battlefields. (I only wonder: if Napoleon hadn't been born, would all those people have died the way they did?)

No, no man, however great, is capable of starting a war – or of preventing one for that matter. Not even God. In truth, how could he be so evil (even if he's above everyone else) to send his people to certain death and suffering, without asking them first? He has other means to achieve the same results. And he has enough diplomacy, when he needs it, to place the blame on the ruler of Abyssinia.

The whole experience of history – says the marquis of Vogue – teaches us that the destruction of war cannot be abolished so long as there are two men alive on this earth, and between them is a loaf of bread and a woman; men will fight to the death for them, rather than sharing both like brothers. There's no better proof of the poverty in the minds of these last three representatives of humankind. The woman, in particular, appears unexpectedly stupid in this fable of Vogue. It's easily seen that the Marquis, however great of a Marquis he was, didn't know women very well.

War is a fatality: it causes itself. This is the idea that those who are in charge of people's happiness and control their destiny dump into our heads with great determination, as if it was an indisputable principle – and they succeeded.

Why then should I write? So that I can pretend that I'm fighting against a fate that belongs, like volcanic eruptions or earthquakes, to the harmony of the universe and to the obscure secrets of our creator? Only because you gave me an advance?

Because in truth, any writer who portrays true scenes from the war, in whatever way he tries to do it, gives the impression that he was against the war. And it's well known now that whoever thinks like this not only doesn't believe in God but also lacks patriotism.

Love for one's country – patriotism – is such a natural and universal emotion that we can say the man who doesn't love his country, the land where he was born and where he grew up, is a man without a soul, a true monster... Now, do I have any reason to be against the war – and to seem like a monster without a soul to others?

If, on the contrary, I declare myself for the war, showing obvious patriotism – I told myself – it's even worse. People would think that I was bragging about my patriotism and that I thought of it as a merit.

To be a patriot is not a merit; it is a duty. Only someone who doesn't find love for his country to be a duty would brag about it. What would we say about a man who bragged out loud everywhere that he loves his wife? We would have a reason not to believe him and to suspect that he loves her less in private than he does in public. Feelings have their own decency.

To be an honest man, to love your country, parents, wife, and not to spit on the street, all of these are the basic duties of any civilized man. Only someone who was not gifted by nature with any special quality can be capable of discovering this worth that costs nothing. I used to know a man who, on the day the political party he supported came to power, asked to be placed in charge of the department of organic chemistry at university, promising that he was a patriot. Another one, long ago, asked to be named director of the National Theater on the grounds that he was a model husband. And he received the appointment.

Now tell me: do I not have worse attributes that I can brag about? If I came to you asking for an advance only because I'm an Orthodox Christian and I love my country, would you have given it to me?

...It's obvious that I can't write anything in Iaşi – I thought to myself – with my mind is so full of doubts and arguments against writing; it's a city that's too loud, too lively, and too full of history. Wherever you look, in the streets, in the public institutions, in the fashion stores – there's history everywhere. Here every stone talks to you of the past and none of the present. So, I'll go somewhere else, where it's quiet and cool, to a place with fewer historical distractions, and perhaps my thoughts will change there.

I ended up at the Văratic monastery – with the nuns. Our Moldavians go there during summer to rest, the men when they have something to work on, and the women when they have nothing to do. There is nowhere more lively than these holy sanctuaries of peace and recollection. First, the nuns have the habit to toll the bells all day and all night. Moldavians – the same. Nuns also have another habit: wooden vesper bells. They beat it in the morning, they beat it at noon, they beat it at midnight… Moldavian women – the same. I had a nun as a host who all day did the same thing, and not only outside – I was curious how there could be so much mysticism in such a small woman.

But especially the big vesper bell from the bell tower, with its jarring sound, had an impact on me contrary to your interests. It reminded me of a machine gun. It was just like I was in Turtucaia all over again. War memories blended in my mind with holy ones, so that I couldn't understand anything anymore…

That's how summer passed and I returned to Iași where, even though it was barely autumn, only early September, I received an invitation from the publishing house to send the manuscript. Which manuscript? What manuscript? I had placed my hope in two-three fragments of memories from my captivity, which I published a long time ago; I would add a few unpublished chapters to them – I told myself – and the book is finished. But when I read them again, I found them so bad that it was as if I hadn't written them. It was like they were written to compromise me, by my unforgettable literary detractor, the critic Eugen Lovinescu.

Someone else in my place would have quickly scribbled down, on the spot, a few dozen pages, as God allowed, and would have escaped from the mess.

But I'm not from Bucharest.

In this regard, people from Bucharest are more efficient; they rush everything – chores, meals, fun, love (on the run like a tit), and they call this living intensely.

We, people from Iași, have another opinion. We don't like to rush, to turn things upside down as they do. When it comes to serious business, we have another habit: we don't do anything.

It's very true, I'm not from Iași (I don't even pretend to be), but I have adapted. Here I found an ambiance that couldn't be more fitting for a professional writer who doesn't like to write. And now you want me to change my view of life? You've got the wrong man. A book is not written like this, as if you'd clap your hands or establish an anonymous stock company; it takes longer than founding a commercial enterprise in our days (that can always go bankrupt in these turbulent times). A good book defies death with its eternity. Policies, bills, contracts – what are these compared to eternity? You businessmen, are dreamers, Mr. Ciornei. You waste your time and fret about things that are as deceptive as shadows and as perishable as grass in the fields. You don't realize that in this earthly life, each member of our generation has a fleeting place, just like sitting on a tram. And if you think more about it, who would be crazy enough to sacrifice his comfort at home, where he lives for a lifetime, focusing all his care and energy on his seat on a tram, where he sits for ten minutes?

In a hundred years, you'll be dead, definitely dead, and immersed in oblivion. All the ministers will be dead as well, even the mayor of the capital, and all the great capitalists of our day, without exception.

Only a good book that you put your name on can raise you above this hecatomb of greatness; and only a writer like me, or another, can offer you this supreme chance. Can't you see what a wonderful business deal I'm offering you?... Disregard the due date set in the contract – and you'll see how happy you'll be after your death. You'll see how happy we'll be two meters underground when we'll know that those above are still reading and enjoying our work.

Because after so much correspondence, emotions, and nuisance on your part, we can say that both of us collaborated on this book: you with the work, me with the capital – that you gave me as a down payment back then.

You caused its conception.

If the critics are unfavorable, I'll take all the blame, but I'll make sure it's a good book. If it will be praised, of course, you'll be solely responsible and culpable for enriching Romanian literature with such a masterpiece.

G.T.

I

24th of August, during the evening…

The enemy machine guns fire across the Danube, from one bank to the other. Under their intermittent bursts, rows of small bubbles appear on the water's surface, popping in the air as if the bullets come from underwater. Successively, around each swimmer, the storm of bullets draws defined circles, that become tighter and tighter, until the head of the man caught in the middle suddenly disappears from sight, just like popping a balloon with a needle…

I wonder what was happening in those heads, the ones visible from here, floating downstream on the waves like minor details? If I had waited for fifteen minutes more in the Danube, I would have known. The hideous death would have snatched me as well, between the sky and the water, without any chance of escape.

In front of us, on the other shore, the train station of Oltenița is burning. A few bombs broke the wall facing us and exploded inside in flashing flames.

A bit lower, a vertical river of black smoke rises fiercely from a petroleum barge that was set on fire.

Here, between the edge of the water and the high bank of sand that still protects them from the Bulgarians' bullets, our people pile up confused. Some of them already tied white flags to the end of their bayonets; others are walking impassively, with hardened souls. For a few hours, the crowd lined up under the banks kept increasing with groups of refugees, most of them without weapons, that came from Turtucaia, hoping to find salvation here across the water or down towards Silistra. But all the boats, planks, and sheaves of twigs are long gone, and the path to Silistra is blocked by the enemy.

How many good swimmers would dare, even in more favorable circumstances, to swim across the Danube? But now, after so many days of fighting and so many sleepless nights, many jumped into the water, barely knowing how

George Topîrceanu in uniform

to swim. Too few had the strength to reach the halfway mark – and they sank. Hundreds and hundreds of others took their place. And the Danube's waves swallowed them in turn, rolling them downstream like ants. The ones the water tossed away by chance, tired but still alive, a few kilometers down on the low banks of the island next to Cosui, the Turks of those places and the old Bulgarians hidden in the bushes pulled them away and hacked them with axes.

Finally, an hour ago, a mounted sergeant appeared from out of nowhere urging the people to resume the attack above the bank.

"No one can shoot the other way, towards Silistra, he said, because the Russians are coming from that direction to help us. Only shoot towards Turtucaia, because the Bulgarians come from that direction…"

I recently came down to the water and I knew very well that it wasn't the way he was saying, but exactly the other way around: the Bulgarians were coming from Silistra and from the south, while our people were coming from Turtucaia.

I watched the man closely. His appearance and accent seemed suspect to me. But it was just an impression that lasted a second… I shouted to those around me not to listen to him because he didn't know what he was talking about. After exchanging some angry words, the sergeant struck me with his eyes and went to grab his revolver... My rifle was faster than his hand and pointed at his heart – and forced him to stop it halfway. Maybe I wouldn't have done it if I knew what was to happen to me two hours later when I was taken prisoner…

After he looked at me closely, as if to remember my face, he slowly withdrew his hand from his revolver, turned his horse around, and got lost in the crowd.

The Bulgarian cannons were now shooting over our heads, towards the road behind the train station that was set on fire, and towards the groves in the direction of the mouth of the Argeş river. In a warehouse not far from the train station, I knew there was a deposit of ammunition for our artillery. It was visible from here that in front of that deposit sat a large pyramid made of bombs waiting to be brought over. One single Bulgarian projectile fallen among them would make many victims among us, all crammed together on the opposite shore in front of them.

Keeping this thought in my head, I stood up from the refuge I had dug in the sand and started walking upstream under the bank.

Groups of disoriented soldiers started to prey on the officer's bags piled up in a cart, especially looking for bottles of cognac. Others with hardened looks, some injured and stained with blood, were swarming everywhere among the carts pulled by local Bulgarians who are looking at the ground somber and horrified, waiting for the events to follow.

An old carrier walked a few steps away from his horses to quench his thirst in the Danube's waters. While he was bent down on his knees at the edge of the water, a gypsy from our group saw him and, in the blink of an eye, took his weapon off his shoulder and shot him in the back of the head. The Bulgarian's body twitched once... then he spread out and remained unmoving face down, with a mustache in the water and the other above it.

"Why did you shoot him?" asked a corporal walking towards him.

"Because he's a Bulgarian!" grinned the gypsy proudly.

Hearing this, the corporal punched him in the face with satisfaction.

"Here!"

And snatching the weapon out of his hand, he threw it in the water:

"This is for being a gypsy," he explained.

Further on...

A few soldiers opened a crate of sugar cubes and emptied it at their feet, on the sand. Before they started to share it among themselves, a gunner with his arm ripped from the elbow, acting crazy, came among them singing church songs. And swinging his stump of an arm that was still hanging from his shoulder, he covered the white pile of sugar with fresh flowing blood.

"Take and eat, as this is the blood that I spilled for you..."

He then collapsed next to the sugar that was abandoned by the disgusted soldiers. He turned pale and his eyes started to fog up.

Next to an open hole in the bank, that was enough to let the carts pass, a few stray Bulgarian bullets whistled past me and hit the water. Four dead soldiers lined up symmetrically in front of the tunnel showed me other bullets hit their target in the same place... A bit further, the blast of a nearby explosion hit me from behind like a fist. I turned my head: a horse from one of the carts I passed a minute ago apparently kicked a grenade buried in the sand. The explosion shattered the front of the cart, killing both horses and the driver.

This is the way things were now. Everyone's life can end with one single step or one simple act you did without even thinking about it. The oblivion wraps you up in its gray web before you even have time to blink. In the past, you believed the illusion that you could clearly see it coming; now nothing is visible, neither ahead nor behind. The past ended and the future has not yet started. We live the uncertain hours between realms, when time itself seems to have stopped, spinning in place like a whirlpool. When this mad reality topples millenary habits and dissolves everything from the inside like a chemical cataclysm, the ones that are faint of heart lose their minds. The instinct of preservation weakens, and every feeling of human solidarity disappears without a trace. Nobody offers to help another anymore. Until not long ago, the dying screams of those drowning, instead of evoking humane feelings in the hearts of those on the shore, caused laughter on their behalf, like witnessing a comedic spectacle.

Death walked among us with her hands behind her back. She enjoyed the aftermath of her great feast like a satisfied courtesan, grabbing a new victim here and there as she pleased. From the pile of crushed corpses to the pontoon above, where panicked soldiers stormed and killed all the injured brought there on stretchers – to here, towards the Kosui-Bulgar village, the whole shore was littered with corpses and agonizing injured soldiers. The Danube's waves kept carrying downstream more and more corpses brought from the city.

In front of me, a few horses stuck in the river mud abandoned by their masters, are agonizing in the middle of this universal indifference. One of them was struggling like an epileptic trying to stand up, but keeps sinking; another one

with a bent neck was barely holding his muzzle above the mud, neighing pitifully asking for help; a third one closer to me lay unmoving on its side, with its
belly swollen with water.

I looked around me, following everything with intense, vivid curiosity.

Lengthy experience with the idea of heinous murder associated it with the
mystery and darkness of the night in people's minds. (Poor petty killings during
times of peace that seized human life every now and then!) But now, war had
crushed even that belief. The horrible scenes of yesterday's attacks unfolded
under the heat of the summer sun when thousands of people were brutally killed
in broad daylight.

How harmless night seemed to me then, wrapping the world in its quiet
darkness – compared to the cruel white light of noon that haunted the air and
showed everyone the hideous emptiness of reality.

The fire of cannons stopped. Rounds of small fires streaming above the
sandy banks sometimes started from upstream and spread along the shore to
here, like a trail of burning ash. The Bulgarians were practicing their shooting
skills using the last moving targets – unfortunate wrecks of human lives – that
the water carried from upstream in front of them…

Six soldiers riding a long log were seen floating down, looking as small as
insects. They frantically paddled with their hands towards the Bulgarian shore
– as a sign that they want to surrender. Their white nakedness, seemingly more
vulnerable without their cloth armor, offered a precise target and attracted
rounds of bullets in their direction. As they got closer, there were only five
left...then four...then three. The last of them lifted his arms in a cross, praying
through a gesture of supreme faith to be spared. But a moment later, he was
gone as well, as if he was pulled down by the unseen hand of an underwater
predator.

Next came a small raft made of branches with three people crouching on it.
As if he was stung from behind by a thorn, the one at the back of the raft stood
up, flailing his arms in the air, and fell in the water like a frog. Losing its weight
from one end, the raft lost its balance and the man crouching on the other end
disappeared in a blink of an eye. Left alone, the man in the middle slipped

through the branches and only his head was visible from the water. And that head floating alone downstream could be heard shouting:

"Brothers!... My brothers!..."

The Danube's surface was finally cleared of the swarm of people that it endured the whole afternoon. With the approaching evening, a strong wind coming from the east started to stir the water, increasing the enmity of the old river that now found its strength again and angrily but majestically rolled its waves downstream. Under the red light of the sun, slabs of heavy and opaque fluid jade rose, staggered, and fell, making its massive flow visible from far away.

...And suddenly, I felt unusual movement around me. A rustling of voices was heard on one side of the group and passed through it.

Every head turned in the same direction, all eyes watching the same thing...

Up, on the top of a round mound, above the path that cut through the bank, a Bulgarian soldier in a brown uniform signaled us with his hat to leave.

It was over.

Over the last act of the bloody battle of Turtucaia, the light curtain of the evening soon fell.

Now the epilogue began.

A long and tragic epilogue, made of countless sinister episodes scattered all over Bulgaria, from Hagifaclar to the bottom of rocky Macedonia. How many of the 25 thousand Romanian peasants that were offered as easy prey to the Bulgarians at Turtucaia will live to see the end of the war and the left bank of the Danube again?...

For the moment, I was concerned with other urgent worries. I now had the right to think only of myself and of how to stay alive.

But what awaited us up there above the banks? A long convoy quickly formed and crawled slowly uphill, but the bayonets of the enemies should have reached their end fifteen minutes ago.

Up, on the top of a round mound, above the path
that cut through the bank, a Bulgarian soldier
in a brown uniform signaled us with his hat to leave

We know Bulgarians hated us to death. We already knew the stubborn phrase that we heard so many times later, like a burden of their simple and primitive hate: *Trinaisi godina*[4] ...

My first concern was that for whatever might happen, I had to hide a small, bulky revolver with six bullets in my back pocket, the last bullet being meant for myself. The first five, I was convinced I'd have time to share unmistakably among my future executioners.

I then thought that if the Bulgarians don't start a carnage but instead choose a certain person to kill, the best thing to do in this situation is to go unnoticed. For that reason, I snatched a pair of well-worn military pants from a cart and pulled them over my new black pants; I put an old hat on my head that I took from a corpse, and I soiled my custom yellow boots on the shore. In another cart, I found a green military coat lined with lamb wool; the Bulgarian carrier that now caught courage and started to believe he was the sole owner of the goods in the cart, prickled at me slightly... but when I stuck my gun under his nose he quickly understood that I don't have time for jokes. In the coat's pockets and sleeves, I stuffed a few first aid items that I made sure to take out of my abandoned suitcase near the water.

Equipped in this way for who knows how long, I finally took my place in the last rows of the big line of soldiers. And throwing one last look at my homelands and the empty shores on the other side of the Danube – I started uphill with determination toward the unknown...

---

[4] 1913.

II

The end of the convoy reached the top of the hill overlooking the river and stopped along a narrow path that was curving between groves towards the Danube. After the given commands reached us, we turned to the left, facing East.

I looked around. Under a mound behind me, there was a small stream that could barely be heard, flowing on a wooden trough. From its end, a thin thread of light arches toward the ground.

And suddenly, a line of Bulgarian riflemen in brown uniforms appeared from out of nowhere twenty paces in front of us...

Holding their weapons ready, they watched us silently.

A voice coming from their direction commanded us to throw down whatever weapons we carried.

From behind them, a few menacing rifles were pointed toward us. During this display of power, one of our officers walked up in front of us frowning, speaking Romanian:

"Praise God!..."

Everyone around me quickly made the sign of the holy cross. Minutes slowly passed, and the pulse of time beat oddly. A few sparrows, readied for the night in a nearby willow, pierced the silence with their indifferent chirps...

Clenching my hand on my revolver, I waited for the first round of bullets to throw myself behind a mound of dirt that I noticed on my left side – and from there, to run back toward the Danube through the reed. That was my one-in-a-thousand chance to escape unharmed...

But the minutes kept passing, and no shot was heard. Maybe it was just an intimidation tactic on their part?...

The lines of Bulgarian soldiers get thicker with a new wave of sweaty and tired fighters, running up the hill from the river: they spoke loudly and walked up front breaking the previous solemnity.

A Bulgarian officer left the right flank and came toward our group holding a revolver in his hand. He walked slowly, watching us...

I recognized him. He's the man I had threatened two hours ago with my rifle when he was riding among us wearing a Romanian uniform. He was looking for me... I stood in the row before last, on the left flank, behind three other people. With a slight movement, I bowed my head and turned my face in the opposite direction. The old soldier cap partially covered my eyes... He passed me. He didn't recognize me. But one single reckless gesture could have betrayed me and cost me my life. Would I encounter him again in the future?

We were signaled to sit down, and the Bulgarians approached us. All of their eyes shone with excitement.

"*Rumanski*! *Rumanski*!"

Some of them came to the spring behind me to quench their thirst. Among them, there was a tanned Bulgarian officer with dusty eyelashes who seemed happier than all of them. He kept laughing and patting our shoulders while his face showed obvious joy.

"*Vous étes heureux d'avoir gagné la bataille,*"[5] one of our soldier told him.

The boy turned around, obviously surprised.

"Oh, no... I'm just happy that we're still alive," he replies in broken French

"But what's going to happen to us?"

"Don't be afraid," replied the Bulgarian. "Our prisoners are treated nicely." "*Ça sera très bien... très bien,*"[6] he added walking away.

At that moment, I started hearing muffled shouts from the right, where a small scuffle occurred. Two Bulgarian soldiers hit one of our officers in the

---

[5] You're happy that you won the battle... (Fr.).

[6] Everything will be good... very good... (Fr.).

head with a gun and left him unconscious and bleeding in a ditch. Another soldier who was thrown out of the line, nobody knew for what reason, was stabbed twice with a bayonet in the back and once in the belly when he fell to the ground. The man squirmed like a worm in the dirt; the Bulgarian soldier tried to pull out his bayonet that was stuck, helped by another man who used his leg for leverage... Other shouts could be heard further away towards the middle of the row; some shouted even further.

By the time we realized what was happening, a strong, commanding voice ordered something in Bulgarian and quieted the rustling of voices and the screams. The Bulgarians went back to their lines, and order was reestablished.

The ones who fell don't get back up. Who knows how many had fallen from our whole group...

Someone communicated to us quietly a rumor saying the fallen men had concealed weapons that were found during a search – and that's why they were executed. It's easily remarked the fact that this was unnecessary. Similar incidents and scenes just as bloody, if not even more horrific, were probably happening along the whole shore – our people had surrendered and were taken prisoners by the Bulgarians. I wondered what was happening in the city...

Sentinels were set on each side of the line, showing us that they were ready to move us. Before I stood up, I pulled the revolver out of my back pocket and buried it in the sand at my feet.

The convoy started moving again, but this time it looked like a herd driven by the will of strangers toward an unknown fate.

Everyone walked along, looking at the ground. Nobody spoke a word anymore. Resignation could be seen on the faces of all the surrounding soldiers – the same docile indifference our peasants have always shown.

The dead and injured were left further and further behind us on the side of the road after this first altercation with the Bulgarians.

On our right, the flaming sunset was slowly vanishing. Through the webs of the evening, I could still see the end of our convoy wherever the road curved, which slowly walked split into two dark rows, like a dark procession of shadows. A quarter pale moon kept up with us from the sky.

***

The part of the convoy that I was in stopped to camp for the night somewhere near an abandoned village next to a small wheat field.

I laid on my back on the smooth and hard ground next to a medic captain that fate chose as my neighbor for that night. We both lit up our cigarettes and started talking quietly. At our feet, the men were sleeping, crammed one next to another to warm themselves up. Some of them were already snoring with their heads under their sheathings.

"Cattle…" my neighbor whispered in disgust. "If they fought how they were supposed to, we wouldn't be here now…"

The doctor was extremely upset about being taken prisoner, he, who believed himself to be safe and sheltered from such a misfortune.

"Look at them sleeping like a bunch of ignorants," he continued resentfully, leaning on his elbow. "It's as if nothing changed in their minds…. as if they just switched masters."

Hearing us talking, a sentinel approached slowly in the dark and leaned to our level, so he could see our faces. He didn't seem to have any hostile intentions. He was a bulky Bulgarian – a grown man with long mustachios who was probably a worthy householder during times of peace.

"*Colco e ceas*?"[7] he quietly asked us with a hint of doubt after examining our expressions.

My neighbor kindly took his watch out and used the light of his cigarette to see the dial... Before getting an answer, the Bulgarian reached with his paw and snatched the watch out of his hand – and slowly walked away from where he came.

"To hell with him," the captain said resentfully after seeing that the man was not coming back. "He stole my watch!"

---

[7] What's the time?

"You must admit he was quite discreet and tactful about it," I said, trying to console him.

"Didn't you have a watch as well? Why didn't you pull it out?"

"I have two, not one. But I had the impression you wanted to answer the question before me..."

Huffing and puffing with envy, the doctor turned his back to me and left me alone with my thoughts.

I stood alone, facing the quiet immersion of the starry sky that seemed to be watching me with its enigmatic gaze through its spidery eyes...

Through the translucent darkness of the August night, I could clearly hear the moans and groans of those who were injured and scattered about every-where. Sometimes I could hear sounds of dogs that were fighting with each other – stray dogs left without a master after the nearby villages were evacuated, that were left to wander in the night among corpses and to stalk the injured. Here and there, shots echoed in the night through the wide ripple of summer's end, followed by sharp yelps.

In the silver clouds of the west, the pearly light of the first quarter braided pale crowns of roses above the world. When this sight of the moon disappeared, the only thing I could see through my eyelashes was the Milky Way, stretched across the sky like a thin wisp of smoke.

***

The cold night and the hard ground underneath me woke me from my sleep. I opened my eyes: the first light was descending upon us... My dreams that I barely broke away from seemed more vivid than the sights of the real world that started taking shape in front of me. An aquarium-like light, dull and green-ish... a gloomy cluster of bodies in various positions – gray faces, wide mouths, arms wrapped between strangers' legs... On a log, near an old shed made of straw and covered in mold on one side, a tired Bulgarian soldier kept watch with his forehead bowed and his gun between his knees.

After the uninterrupted roaring of cannons from yesterday and the days be-fore, this overwhelming silence seemed supernatural. I had the impression that

I was alone in the middle of a universe that had been forever numbed. Even the leaves of the nearby mulberry seemed to be set in a miraculously frozen state.

There was a rustling... a dog appeared between two bushes, sneaking and walking at a ghostly pace. Its whole head was smeared with blood, from its muzzle to its ears. He remains still for a few moments, standing on three legs and sniffing us from afar... then it turned around and disappeared quietly like a shadow.

From the opposite direction came another dog, bigger, with a full belly. He stopped and looked at us with the placid eyes of a satisfied animal. When his eyes met mine over the pile of sleeping bodies, I saw a strange ferocious light in his eyes, and the hair on his back stood up, as if I was a wolf...

III

A long journey under the sun, in the late summer's heat...

I was not aware of how many days had passed since we had begun marching south. We kept walking further into Bulgarian lands and further away from our country.

The harsh and poor lands rarely gave way to villages. We camped wherever night found us, near a village, on the side of the road, in a field...

The locals were bitter towards us. In a place, in the vicinity of the battlefield, a whole village chased us with axes and scythes. To avoid a general scuffle that would have been dangerous for everyone, our escorts were forced to bar the way with their bayonets.

The guides escorting us – called *ciasovoi* in Bulgarian, who were under the command of *starşi*[8] – were replaced almost daily. The further away we walked from the front, the more diverse our escorts became; the uniforms and the discipline disappeared gradually – and the guides become meaner and greedier. Every new change of escorting guards plundered on the prisoners, especially on the officers, for anything that hadn't already been taken. They stole openly with no fear of repercussions. If an unfortunate soldier tried to resist, he was either stabbed with a bayonet or hit in the chest with the gun until he fell into a ditch, foaming at the mouth.

The ones that left their spot during the march suffered the same fate: the *ciasovoi* attack them as if they were savage sheepdogs, screaming at them, or throwing clubs at them as if they were cattle if they couldn't reach them.

---

[8] Sub-officers.

For four days, our people had nothing to eat. The Bulgarians didn't even feed us a slice of bread up to then. The first words we learned from them were *utre*, which means *tomorrow*, and *ciacă* – meaning *wait!*

But the thirst that tormented us was worse than the hunger because, after a while, we stopped feeling it. We could hardly find any water when we camped in a village. Wells were scarce in this barren land. After being used by so many troops and convoys, they had dried up almost completely. The buckets sometimes only brought up mud from the bottom of the wells. In order to share enough water for each man, we had to delay our journey for many hours each day. That's why when we reached a well, the guards were posted in front of it to block people from reaching the water. They rushed toward it anyway from fear of death.

A true battle took place over a wild apple tree near a road when the convoy passed by it. There were dead and injured like on the battlefield. Crazed by thirst and hypnotized by a few small apples left on the high branches of the tree, the people left their line, hung on the branches, threw rocks at them, and fought each other like wolves over a withered apple fallen in the dirt. Nothing could stop them, not even the guards' shouts or the sight of those who lay in the dirt, their heads smashed in by guns.

I gambled with my life as well a few days before, for a jug of water – so I wouldn't die of thirst along the way.

This happened on the first day of our journey after we came across the first well, and the Bulgarians didn't let us approach it. By that time, I had been without water since the evening before. The sun was starting to burn. I was thinking about how I forgot to take a jug of water when I was rushing to get ready. I didn't suspect we would lack this – how was that supposed to cross my mind when I had the Danube right next to me? But now I realized that a mistake like this could have been fatal.

What was I supposed to do?

On that day, we crossed the border at Daidir, through the lands where the battle took place. Corpses were scattered everywhere – people had been shot while they were running away shortly after the trenches had fallen into Bulgarian hands. I knew that some corpses had to have jugs of water on them, kept on hooks alongside their bags of bullets.

I had my eyes on a corpse, near the side of the road. He lay on his side in the same position a rifle or a grenade had left him. As soon as I walked by him, I left my line after the guard passed me, and in a blink of an eye, I was next to the corpse... Disaster: the jug was secured with a hard leather belt. I tugged, I pulled... but the corpse didn't feel like parting with it. In that rigid body, a sense of propriety still remained. But after I risked my life for it, I didn't want to drop the plunder from my hand. And the dead man silently fought me, desperately hanging on to this last link he had with life, crawling after me a few paces... Finally, the belt broke – and I managed to take my place in line before the guard noticed I was gone.

I had my own jug to fill up for the journey. Even better, it was almost full.

I let others drink from that water because there were injured people among us, who started being tortured from the first day as if they were damned in hell.

When we started marching on that first day, our injured that were left on the road overnight (because the Bulgarians only helped their own people), seeing the long prisoner convoy that was walking south guarded by bayonets, understood what was happening... they stood up however they could, staggering, and they were coming to us from every direction trying to see us for the last time. Some of them had wounded legs, and they were crawling on their elbows to reach the road – they were begging to be taken as well, not to be left alone with the Bulgarians who were on their way there. Others who had minor injuries entered the lines without being seen and joined us.

Among those closest to me, there was a man with a hole in his chest, his right lung pierced by a bullet that left an exit wound on his back. He walked, supporting himself on the shoulder of his neighbor – he spit blood with every step he took.

"Can you still walk?"

"I can..."

He somehow reached Razgrad.

As soon as I walked by him, I left my line
after the guard passed me, and in a blink of an eye,
I was next to the corpse...

Another had a wounded hand. A splinter from a projectile sliced his thumb at the base. He bandaged the wound himself with a dirty handkerchief. The bloody cloth dried up and stuck to his wound – but it got wet again and dripped when he let his hand drop to his side. So he was forced to walk holding his hand up, pale and somber as if he carried his own funeral candle.

The ones who fell, who remained behind, were lost. The Bulgarians didn't have carts available for our wounded men. Why would they bother with them, transport them, and treat them in their hospitals? To get rid of them they found a faster method: they shot them. Those who got shot could pretend they died on the battlefield like so many others a few days earlier. Who would account for them?

In the Balbunar forest, the sub-officers on duty organized a great theft, unheard of until then. They laid out a tent sheet on which every passing prisoner had to throw everything of value in his possession. The poor man who was caught hiding something...

I couldn't do anything about it, because I was constrained to do it as well. I had it easy until then – the clothes that partially disguised me and the green beat-up coat I carried under my arm inside out to make it look like it was a torn tunic, didn't raise anyone's suspicion. But now I had to give something, so they wouldn't search me. When my turn came, I gave them a cheap Turkish watch, that I had bought as a souvenir in Turtucaia ten days prior. Showing off such a luxury item like this was unwise, but I didn't have another item that I could easily part with.

"Where did you get this?" asked one of the officers who spoke a bit of Romanian.

"I stole it from an officer," I replied.

The Bulgarian laughed, then turned to the one coming up behind me – and I got away with it. If he had thought about searching me, he would have had a big surprise; aside from other items of low value for them (two soaps, a toothbrush, a small volume of Vigny, a "Gillette" razor – and other curiosities), I had another watch, a small gold ring, and a few hundred lei[9] in silver coins, scattered through all my pockets.

In the morning, shortly before we reached Razgrad, I noticed a few school boys in uniform among the Bulgarians who were escorting us. They had been sent before the first light to greet us and guard us for this last portion of the journey. Silent and grave, they now walked next to us on the side of the road, impressed by the seriousness of the mission that was given to them, each carried an old rifle, much too heavy for their young shoulders. I tried to speak to one of them in French. He came to me and seemed very kind and decent. He had a hard time speaking French, but he seemed excited to be able to practice his language skills.

"Me and my colleagues are from Razgrad," he said. "We were ordered to guard you, so you don't run..."

"Can you shoot?"

"A bit..."

He felt the need to add more to that:

"Bulgaria has been at war for four years, and there are not many people left. We also have to do our duty. There's a teacher here with us..."

"Among the escorts?"

"Yes."

He went to look for him. They both came to me. The teacher was dressed in civilian clothes, with dusty white shoes. We talked for a few miles. He was a French teacher, and he seemed to be a highly cultured man. There was no enmity from him about the Quadrilateral, towards the *trinaisi godina*...

"Our people didn't expect to take so many prisoners," he told me, "they weren't ready to feed so many so fast. Where are they supposed to get thousands of loaves of bread in such a short time?"

---

[9] Romanian currency.

When I recounted to him everything that happened to us along the way, he became upset:

"This is war, my friend. There's nothing that can be done about it. The escort is made of various types of people. But after you reach Sofia, when you get into regular camps, things will change."

"What part of the country are we being taken to?"

"Probably to Macedonia."

"On foot?"

"Not all the way. From Razgrad there will probably be multiple convoys, going in different directions. Anyway, I advise you to not meddle with the officers, it's best to stay with the soldiers..."

IV

We reached Razgrad.

We walked along the oriental-looking streets of the city's outskirts amid a dusty stampede of loose dogs and barefoot children who ran around us and threatened us with their fists. Housewives ran to the gates to see us and they shouted for their neighbors to come out as well.

The convoy moved slowly, and the men could barely stand up. They were not interested in the houses or the markets we passed along the way. They didn't care about anything anymore. Skinny, dirty, and hungry, with their faces sunken in, and glassy eyes, as if they were from another world, all dragging their feet without looking anywhere around them.

The locals had a hostile attitude toward us. Crowds of people followed us and in some places, we were greeted by an uproar, booing, whistles, and insults:

"Boo! *Rumanski*!... *Trinaisi godina*!"

Everything was too much. After the absurd events that fate kept tormenting us with for the past few days, this anger toward these pitiful starved men looked almost comical to me. It was like a perversity of inanimate objects that surpassed the comprehension of those surrounding me. A militiaman from the back of the convoy that was looking down and barely dragged his feet suddenly awakened from his daydream:

"I wonder what their problem is with us? Tell me these people aren't stupid…"

Losing hope that we'd find bread and water, some were starting to sway and fall just as we were about to reach our next stop.

At the corner of a street, a short, fat Bulgarian woman, red in the face with chubby cheeks, threw insults at our people while showing her backside:

"*Ptiu, rumanski*! Na!... Ptiu, *rumanski*!

Among the spews she throws out a pornographic word in our language, probably the only one she learned for this special occasion. All the men got to hear it as they passed by her.

"Look at this bitch," grumbled the man next to me, extremely annoyed, with his forehead wrinkled in a frown. "If I had a choice," he said in a hungry voice in an outburst of offended manhood, "I would take her by her braids and throw her to the ground."

We stopped at the edge of the city in a valley. We stood in the sun like a big group of nomads. The ground and the grass were trampled, with visible signs of stakes and tents. You could tell that other troops had passed through here before us.

There was no shade anywhere. The midday sun was scorching the top of our heads.

There was an old well with a shaduf at the end of the camp. Around it, there was a swarm of men who were shoving and fighting each other. Overgrown with bodies hanging on it, the well sometimes disappeared like a bee in the middle of an angry swarm of flies. The shaduf kept frantically going up and down, with no moment of respite, with a screech resembling that of a wounded beast. The bucket that was snatched from every direction and hit on the well's walls only brought up a sort of thick, black soup that the lucky ones handling it must scoop in their hands from the bottom. They mostly eat it rather than drink it.

I got out of the crowd to breathe freely. Bulgarians are practical people with the spirits of merchants. Some locals thought that the prisoners might have money left – they came with water jugs, cakes, or melons. But there was no way to sell anything because the sentries didn't let anyone near the camp or have any contact with us. I managed, however, to throw a silver coin to a woman from whom I received, thrown through the air like a soccer ball, a green melon to quench my thirst. I thought its sour pulp might help with hunger as well after so many days without food.

When I was about to get up, one of the curious Bulgarians who came to see us called me and signaled my way. He was the French teacher from Razgrad who had time to go home and now was looking for me for who knows how long. He walked past the sentinels and ran toward me. He brought me a loaf of bread, but we quickly needed to part ways:

"*Adieu, mon ami...et bonne chance*,"[10] he wishes me, shaking my hand warmly.

This was life in times of war. Farewells were sudden, and often, they're forever. But I would have liked to see this man again, even if only in the after-life.

"See?" said one of the men that I shared my bread with, with his mouth full and chewing. "Not all Bulgarians have cold hearts as we thought."

"There are boyars among them once in a while," added another man, trying to stuff a few leftover crumbs into his mouth.

"Of course!"

Those who lost their lives were pulled to the edge of the camp without delay. As soon as a man dies, two other men are ready to grab him by his head and legs and carry him past the sentinels, a hundred steps away, near a fence. Many were ready for this task knowing that if they found a way to that part of the camp they might find someone that sells water or bread.

These mortuary transportations were frequent, but the pile of bodies didn't seem to be growing.

Suddenly, two officers who started to suspect something, jumped two people carrying a body and attacked them with clubs without a moment's notice. Seeing the danger, the two carriers dropped the body and ran back, followed by their attackers.

Left alone in the middle of the road, the corpse lifted his head, looked around him, and measured the distance... then he quickly stood up and ran away.

The officers were left confused.

---

[10] Goodbye, my friend... and good luck! (Fr.).

– Da eb ,aika! Rumanski!... they curse in Bulgarian while trying to catch the "corpse."

The noon sun had passed overhead a long time ago. The sound of the well could be heard constantly. People didn't have any patience anymore, they were walking and fussing all over the camp. Nobody liked to stay in one place for too long. Wry faces, sunken eyes – the need for food was imprinted on every-one's faces. They were all waiting for the same thing.

"Bread, *gospodin*! *Hleb*!" shouted a man at the edge of the camp to a nearby officer, signaling him by moving his fingers to his mouth.

"Wait!" replied the Bulgarian.

But hours passed and hopes for a loaf of bread disappeared with the sun that sunk under the horizon, wrapped in a wide aura of pink light.

Most men lay there discouraged facing up – they barely had any strength to talk to each other. A low murmur of voices was heard from this sea of hungry men. In the agony of twilight, the long screech of the tired well was heard less and less, signaling that the black milk had dried up and the shaduf was frozen in the air, like a long reptile neck from another era.

The part of the city visible to us was now lit up by joyful lights. A wide dark space separated us from it.

The lights reminded us of the sweet and comfortable life we once had. Here a foreign world impassively followed its usual routine. On this side of the city, a group of wrecked men was suffering in the dark, isolated, as if they were on an island in this foreign land. Over this sea of loneliness made up of the com-bined feelings of every man, and fragile cells of humanity, thoughts, and un-spoken nostalgia, the Milky Way shone its thin spectral light.

What mysterious destiny awaited each of us? No one knew. From the first step we took on enemy territory, each of us felt as if a new war had started, one that was harder than the one we had just escaped from. The war of each of us against everyone else – against people and weather, against hunger and cold, diseases, and unforeseen events – the war of each of us against the whole universe. In this fight, you can't rely on sacrifices from your people who are just as threatened as you are. You're alone with your own resources that you can't waste on others if you want to live. Like the pilot of a plane without an engine, you must use every breeze to land as late and as far as possible.

V

The road stretched again in front of us, through an infinite desolation of poor lands and harsh rustic monotony, under the early autumn light.

On the morning before leaving Razgrad we were each given a loaf of bread. The great convoy was then reassembled on the road facing east. We knew that it was going to be split into multiple convoys and sent in different directions. Which one should I join? Toward what faraway camp? On what long and unknown journey would each of us go? It depended entirely on luck. I joined the front of the first convoy on the side of the camp. The officers signaled us to start walking with their usual cry:

"Come on!"

And everyone slowly started walking with their usual absent-minded faces.

As soon as we walked away from the city, the plundering started again. The officers were worse than ever – a type of Bulgarian Turk, wearing the typical large woolen pants held up by a braided belt, and wearing a small white cap on the top of their heads, similar to what our merchants of old used to wear.

This time, our people were robbed of coats. Shouts and screams could be heard all along the convoy while the plundering was taking place. If two or three officers noticed a coat they like, they jumped the man without warning and snatched it out of his hands. The man held on to it desperately, knowing that without it he would shiver every night from then on, he would freeze, and die of cold before the end of autumn. But in the end, under a rain of punches, he was forced to give it up.

The coats taken in this way were then sold for cheap or traded for brandy to the locals from the surrounding villages who followed the convoy for business.

During the night stop, the drunk officers kept shooting toward the sky for fun. And they misfired several times, shooting toward the middle of the crowd. Isolated screams of wounded men replied, woken up from their sleep. Some of them died this way, maybe during a deceiving dream that made them feel as if they were at home with their families...

I only have sparse and confused memories of these events. I was sick. On the morning of the following day, I walked for miles with my eyes closed and using the shoulder of someone next to me for support; I was running a fever, and my head was spinning.

I remember that during a rainy evening, our convoy stopped near a small town, behind a train station, in a pen made of barbed wire. We stayed in the rain all night. We had to stand up because the ground was muddy.

In the morning, when the rain stopped, and the sun came up, a group of locals came to see us. From far away they started hurling rocks at us, over the sentries' heads... I remember we were ready to break through the chain of sentinels and jump the group of rascals that was savagely attacking us.

To keep us away from their patriotic fury, the officers stuffed us in a few freight wagons that were stationed on an unused railway and left us there behind locked doors. The sun was heating the metal walls and the roofs of the wagons which started to cook us like an oven. We all felt like we were going to collapse from the heat. I was sweating.

In the evening, when the air cooled off, we were taken out of those iron prisons and moved into other wagons that had no roofs.

The locomotive was ready to start.

I sat on a platform with my legs hanging out. A few minutes after the train started to move, I started feeling as if my whole body was immersed in icy water. My fever broke. I laid on my back and rested my head against a group of people. A deep and restful sleep isolated me from reality and lasted uninterruptedly until the next day.

When I opened my eyes in the morning, it was already daylight. The train had stopped at a small station at the foot of the mountains.

We passed the Balkans.

Our men still slept huddled together on the open platform of the wagon convoy. In the sharp morning light, the spectacle of this crowd of bearded men who seem to have come from the edge of the world, dusty and dirty after passing through many blackened tunnels filled with clouds of black smoke, reminded me of a gray surreal painting, seen through the lens of a spyglass. A few of them woke up and went to drink clean water from a pump at the end of the train station. But none of them thought about washing even a bit: it was probably too cold for it…

After the sentinel allowed it, I hopped off the wagon and went there. I felt nimble and whole – maybe just a bit weak – but no sign of the chills I had over the past two days. I took my clothes off and cleaned myself in a rush with the soap and the shaving blade hidden in my pockets. After a few minutes of haggling, I bought a black wool hat from a local; I threw the old cap away together with the other torn clothes I had worn until then, which I had also used as a disguise.

The officers were watching me amazed by this sudden transformation that was taking place under their eyes, but none of them bothered me in any way, probably too curious to see what happened at the end.

"*Ciorbagiu, bre! Rumanski ciocoi…*"[11]

"*Ti se ofiţir?*[12] …" asked one of them frowning

"*Niet!*"[13] I answered

---

[11] You're rich, man! Romanian boyar!

[12] Are you an officer?

[13] No!

And to cover my loss, he gave me his
wooden cigarette box so that I could roll one for myself

And I climbed back onto the platform and took my place, so I don't miss the train.

"Why did you tidy yourself like a maiden?" grumbled an envious voice from the crowd. The one who spoke was a bulky man with cow eyes who was crouching between other men to get warm, looking dirtier than everyone else combined... People like him think that during war or other similar circumstances, you must walk around unwashed and dressed in the same dirty clothes as they do to please them.

We reached Sofia at sunrise.

A train from the opposite direction, either an accelerated or an express train was blocking us from view. Nobody was allowed to get off the train.

I gave the officer guarding my wagon a two-lei coin:

"Cigarette, *gospodin*... Tobacco!"

And I signaled him to go buy me some.

"*Ne moje*,"[14] replied the Bulgarian grinning in a friendly manner. But he took my coin and stuffed it in an old leather sachet at his waist. And to cover my loss, he gave me his wooden cigarette box so that I could roll one for myself. That was the first time I tried Bulgarian tobacco, cut very thin but spicy, and their cigarette sheets that were almost transparent like they were made of butter.

"*Oşti edna...*" The surprisingly kind Bulgarian urged me to roll another one.

Through the light and cold fog of the morning, one of their superiors walked along the wagons shouting in Romanian:

"Those who know their way around canons, get down and come with me!"

"What does he want with artillerymen?"

In a moment I was ready to get down. But then I thought this couldn't be any special treatment on their part. They might have some other reason to call us.

---

[14] It's not possible...

A young woman appeared at the door of a wagon
– a high-class Bulgarian or maybe a foreigner

"Don't go," one of the soldiers mirrored my thoughts out loud. "Don't worry, they are not calling us out to serve us pie…"

(In truth, I found out later that those who answered the call of the Bulgarians were taken back to Turtucaia and asked to show them where they had hidden the sighting devices and canon locks. It was said some were thrown into the Danube to pull them out after they admitted to throwing them in the water. After what they suffered at their hands, a few of them returned to camp to tell us what they had endured).

The same Bulgarian walked among us a few hours later looking for two craftsmen of any kind: blacksmiths, masons, carpenters.

This time I regretted not knowing such a craft. I would have had the chance to stay in Sofia, instead of being taken to unknown places, away from any city for who knows how long.

Our convoy was ready to start traveling again. The officers got in the wagons.

Gloomy faces watched us from behind the curtains of the luxury wagons at the front.

A young woman appeared at the door of a wagon – a high-class Bulgarian or maybe a foreigner. She was dressed in a tight gray suit that showed her curves. She pulled off one of her gloves to lift her veil above her long eyebrows; her polished nails look like jewels, glittering in the sun. Her slightly shadowed blue eyes looked across the groups of prisoners, with a slow, grave, and indifferent look…

I looked at her and tried to imprint her image on my retina so I could hold on to this last graceful vision of delicate feminine beauty that chance had brought my way. I thought that it would be a long time until I would get to meet an authentic civilized woman – the female companion of the modern man – whom nature and art turn into a complete masterpiece from head to toe. I was grateful to this stranger for unknowingly giving me this opportunity…

Her gaze stopped on me, slightly surprised. In a sudden unrestrained gesture, I quickly pulled out the ring that I saved from the disaster of the previous days and throw it at her feet.

The stranger saw it. The line between her eyebrows deepened, and her blue eyes pierced me angrily from underneath her lashes. But seeing the plea and the true sentiment that urged me to do this, she bent down and picked it up from near the wagon stairs.

While our trains were departing in opposite directions, she smiled at me, and her white hand gave me a friendly farewell with her glove.

VI

A Décauville locomotive pulling an endless row of small roofless wagons brought us here from Radomir, on the north side of the Rhodope Mountains. The black skeletal mountains that look almost barren, with sharp cliffs and peaks made of burnt stone looked like they belonged to another planet… When you look at them you feel like your soul was empty, your head starts hurting, and you get a feeling of dread, mixed with sinister thoughts about the nothingness of this earthly life.

The railway ends here. The world ends here. Tonight we slept on the platforms, or in the wagons that carried gravel and sand before they carried prisoners. Tomorrow morning we start on foot through the mountains, downstream Struma river, to cross into Macedonia, the other realm.

The terminus station was a simple wooden warehouse with a new roof made of boards, similar to the other stations where this toy train stopped before arriving here. Two lonely households can be seen further away, probably the homes of poor peasants. We could see Struma bending on the right – which I saw for the first time – that curves its waves like a giant constrictor snake laying in the shade, under the mountain showing its sharp fangs.

Shortly after our arrival, a small group of twenty or thirty foreign prisoners stopped next to the warehouse. They were probably brought here from the lower part of the mountains.

"They might be Italian or French," explains one of our men. "Can't you see how rough they're being treated by the Bulgarians?"

We jumped on the platforms to stretch our legs, and I went to visit these brothers in arms whom fate brought our way.

They were French, captured on the Thessaloniki battlefield. It seems they were caught recently, as they weren't yet used to the habits of the Bulgarians. I tried to talk to them, and I told them that we were Romanians. After we exchanged a few words, they asked me if our people have any food. They were starving, poor people. And they were angry that the Bulgarians gave them nothing so far:

"*Ces bougres-là! Sont-ils assez emmerdants avec leur ciaka et utre... nom de Dieu!*"[15]

Ciaca and *utre*... We know that.

We were each given a warm loaf of bread in Radomir before we left, freshly out of the oven. But no matter how much you searched for it, not even a crumb was left by now.

A cat showed up on the fence of a Macedonian household that seemed abandoned. The French saw it, and in the blink of an eye they organized themselves to capture it, some on one side and some on the other. They trapped it in a semicircle that started to tighten around it. The cat was lying in the sun on the fence, not realizing what was about to happen. And you're supposed to believe that animals have instincts. A French man approached it slowly, not giving it a reason to get scared – and then he suddenly smashed its head with a piece of wood that he had hidden behind his back. He took it off the fence... He crouched over it for a few moments doing something; then, he lifted it by its tail and came back proudly.

The Bulgarians were laughing.

Our people watched the events from afar, with their hands behind their backs. They first thought the people were just having fun, something their nation normally does. Maybe they thought they have a habit of killing cats to pass the time.

When they saw the foreigners light up a fire, while others were skinning the cat and pulling out its insides, they started to suspect that something was wrong.

"I wonder what they're planning to do with it?"

---

[15] Those bastards! They're so irritating, my God, with their *ciaka* and *utre*! (Fr.).

The French chopped up the cat in equal pieces and threw them in a metal pot to boil. Our people watched – and it seemed as if they still didn't believe what they were witnessing... Only at the end, when they saw them sharing the soup, each receiving a small bowl with a piece of meat and some broth, they turned around disgusted and spit.

"Did you see that?... What a foul nation!"

"They're boyars... they don't want to eat all from the same pot..."

At Radomir, a *potporucic*[16] gave me a few commanding attributes that raised my rank among them. (I'm in charge of discipline, I can assist in sharing the bread, I can ask for wellness measures to be taken when we halt, etc.)

The first thing I asked the sentry was to let the people take turns and bathe in the Struma river.

I thought they would all rush to it. But too few followed my example when I was the first one to get undressed and take a cold bath. They didn't trust these foreign waters flowing angrily, which seemed to bubble in Bulgarian, even if their color was the same as our waters.

As I was getting dressed, a man who was washing his face upstream stopped and shouted, looking toward the water:

"Where are you going?"

Being the only two people left there, I looked in that direction to see who he was talking to but I didn't see anyone.

"Can you hear me? Where did you go?..." the one on the shore shouts again, blocking the sun with his hand.

I followed his gaze but I still didn't see anyone.

"Who are you talking to?" I asked.

"You didn't see him? One of our men swam on the other side..."

"You must have imagined it."

---

[16] Second Lieutenant.

In truth, there was plenty of daylight left – the sun was barely setting behind the mountain – and the Struma didn't seem a lot wider than our Olt river. If a man tried to escape by swimming across it, it would be impossible for me not to see him.

The man I spoke to slowly returned to the wagons. He must have been hallucinating because of exhaustion and weakness.

I let him leave, so I could be alone for a few minutes and enjoy the water and the quiet of twilight. Sitting there with my back to the camp, I could imagine I wasn't a prisoner anymore. I could imagine that I was free. And I was trying to extend these moments of peace and loneliness as much as possible – because after so many days of forced promiscuity, the need for physical isolation, for being alone only for a few minutes, was tormenting me more than hunger.

Not much time had passed and a sentry came looking for me and returned me to the camp. He kept telling me something on the way in his language, but I couldn't understand anything. Only when I reached the camp I understood what was happening.

A man had died.

I found him in the corner of a wagon, resting his back against the edge of the platform, with his chin on his knees – he looked as if he was sleeping. He was a small, slim man, with his face sunken in and his mustache trimmed. Nobody knew where he was from or what his name was.

"He ate warm bread and his heart failed," one of our people tried to explain to the Bulgarian soldiers in Romanian.

"*Cacvo* heart?"[17] The Bulgarian asked frowning.

This was how things were now. The trials we had to face made a terrible selection among people. The weak died one by one. It was enough for the body to be damaged even a little bit – and the whole life could drain out of it shortly.

---

[17] Which, what type?

"Look, this is the man I saw crossing the river earlier when I was washing," said a voice behind me. "I know him well, I saw him swimming with my own eyes…"

"Yeah right," answered another man from the same wagon. "He hasn't moved from that spot since this morning."

"When did he die?" I asked.

"Not long ago, at sunset…"

He died the minute the man on the shore saw him in the middle of the river, swimming to the other side...

VII

Macedonia, a mountain country filled with shepherds and warrior fieldworkers, painted brown on the map of Europe; the tangled geography that used to horrify me in school and cause me to fail... A land blessed by God with thorns and stones, where I didn't imagine I'd end up, not even in my worst dreams... Macedonia, a land with a rich historical past where ancient civilizations used to live once, that came here from the top of the mountains and left through its valleys like a small river, leaving no drop behind it; an amphitheater of cliffs shaken by earthquakes, a nest of endemic anarchy, a blend of enemy nations, each more brachycephalic than the other, that tore each other apart with their teeth for so many years, and violated each other, until they ended up getting fused together. *Homo Balkanicus* – a unique race on the face of the Earth that is European by geographic definition and its birthplace... Macedonia, a province with towns as big as a palm and villages hung like magpie nests on the cliffs, so they don't get robbed. You can't reach them either by cart or by plane, only by riding donkeys and risking getting thrown down into an abyss; a country with clean and patriarchal habits, where a woman caught cheating is stabbed on the spot and chopped up like a lamb, for offending her traditions and her ape of a husband.... Macedonia... fresh pastures on high planes from the Mosquito Kingdom; peaks the color of coal from where you can see thin rivers sparking like mercury and curving through barren valleys; an opaque porcelain sky, milky on its zenith and azure at the horizon... blue mornings and long golden sunsets... hot afternoons under a cannibalistic sun that shines its chalky light over rows of burnt rock and low hills made of dry dirt that is sparsely covered with thin grass...

Maybe Macedonia didn't resemble the way I'm describing it here. But what choice did it have? This is the perception I had of it that might be influenced by the fact that I wasted a few months of my life in captivity here...

Actually, from an objective point of view, Macedonia is even worse.

The mountains are more arduous than I described above; the towns are smaller, the villages are poorer; sunsets are not that golden, sometimes they're the color of cooked carrots; not even the habits of locals are that austere – women cheat, especially during war...

We descended between the peaks of the Rhodope mountains following the Struma downstream, under Rila-Planina, on barren paths with no vegetation. Every once in a while you could see a few rusty ferns and small bunches of juniper that seemed to be watching us as we passed by; a few mountain blue-bells sparkled here and there in the shade of the bare cliffs.

We sometimes walked over small rivers on tall wooden bridges built by the Germans and the prisoners. Every bridge had a German inscription with the date it was built. The Germans left the Bulgarians many such useful gifts, as a reminder of their passing through these poor lands; all hold the mark of their technical craftsmanship being left for the locals to use as a token of civilization and true and constructive patriotism. In one spot on a shore, I saw a huge effigy of the Kaiser that was sculpted in solidified sand. We walked before it – and each of our poor people blessed it with a curse in appreciation.

Heavy truck convoys were catching up behind us, loaded with provisions and ammunition; others would greet us from the opposite direction, loaded with wounded men, a sign the battlefield was not far away. When we left the mountains, close to Gorna-Giumaia and Crivo-Livada, we finally started hearing the cannon blasts from Thessaloniki, resounding like a weak storm in the distance.

We left behind us the golden beginning of autumn; here we fell under intense sunlight, white and hot as in the middle of summer – the heat rose as we continued walking south.

***

One evening we finally stopped at the edge of a prison camp – a cluster of small shelters spread on a thin bank above the Struma river, like some primitive African huts, made of dry willow and alder branches.

At sunset, when we arrived there we were taken into custody by a Bulgarian camp commander who called me over for a private discussion, probably to instruct me about the discipline and the living arrangements in this crowded colony of prisoners. But who could understand anything that came out of his mouth? Only *scrrrr...* and *pîrr* and *rabota* and *scîrscăta* – it seemed a miracle to me how a normal man could speak in such a way without spitting all his teeth in the grass. He even had mustachios resembling thick hemp, that would slur his words, and above all else, he had a big curved nose, with straight nostrils, that looked like a two-barrel pistol.

Paralyzed by the sight of that nose that distracted my attention the whole time, I quietly listened without understanding a word he was saying, while the Bulgarian glared at me and shouted like I was deaf to make me understand. In the end, he looked me in the eyes and shouted:

"*Răzbirăşi?*"

In our language, it meant "Did you understand?" or more precisely, "Did your mind manage to comprehend what I said?..."

In the general metaphysical way of things maybe it wasn't that hard to understand by God's grace; I couldn't understand the language very well but I could understand an idea here and there.

To not embarrass myself further I shouted back at him:

"*Scîrscătă!*"

And went on to mind my own business.

There were many nationalities among the prisoners – French, Italians, Greeks, Montenegrins, and especially Serbians – aside from the Bulgarians who were in charge of guarding us. To complete the cosmopolitan look of this diverse camp, a few English found themselves lost there, even though they had a separate camp close to Sofia, which was said to be more comfortable than the rest of them.

Because it was quite cold during the night, and we didn't have time to build shelters for ourselves when we arrived, we asked our foreign comrades to host our people in their huts for a night. The Italians and the French refused the hospitality, probably bothered by the unkempt look of these fresh allies coming from across the Danube. However, the Serbians received them with open hearts.

The next day our people were not asked to work with the others – they were given a day off to build shelters.

At noon, when the other prisoners returned for their hour-long break, the leader of the Serbians – who spoke Romanian, being born in the valley of Timoc – came to me frowning and told me:

"Listen Romanian... last night we hosted your people like they were our brothers. From today on, if we find a Romanian near our huts, we'll stab them..."

I wondered what had happened. When they returned from work, the Serbians noticed their overnight guests abused their trust. Things were missing from every hut...

Hearing of this incident, the Bulgarian commander took us a hundred meters away from camp, as if we had the plague, and ordered us to build our huts there, commanding the sentinels not to let us trespass in the camp.

We started our new lives in the camp under these happy circumstances, surrounded by love and consideration.

The reason the prisoners were stationed here was to help the German occupation build a new Décauville railway on a certain sector. The work started in multiple locations at once, along the whole Struma Valley, from Demir-Hissar to our camp. Therefore, multiple isolated parts of the railway were being built at the same time, which were meant to meet in the future and connect. By winter, this railway that was completely built by prisoners will have had to connect Sofia-Küstendil and the center of Bulgaria with the battlefield in Thessaloniki.

Our people were leaving every morning to work about 2 miles away, escorted by sentries. I was left alone in the camp. At five in the afternoon, I'd go escorted by a few carriers to take provisions for the next day – a few small loaves of black bread, sometimes crumbly biscuits, tomatoes, peppers, and beef or sheep meat twice a week. Two cooks, who were being switched weekly, were cooking soup in a cauldron. During the evening we shared the bread for the following day.

The prisoners were stationed here to help the German occupation build a new railway

The drinking water was bad. The Struma River was contaminated with cholera. The Germans had made small pumps at regular distances from each other in the valley, by digging in the rocky ground and planting thin pipes, from which stale rusty water came out that felt like it was burning our throats. Because of it, men avoided them and secretly drank water straight from the river – but none of them got cholera.

Sundays were the days when everyone could rest. Our men spent the whole day lying down – they barely even talked to one another. They were more tired, discouraged, and dirtier than their foreign captive brothers.

The other camp was more animated. The Italians were singing, the French were talking, and the Russians – because we were followed in camp by a few of them – talked all day about politics and made plans for everyone. Only the four Englishmen sat alone on a log smoking their pipes and not speaking for hours.

The Serbians were always dealing with their huts. Held as captives for longer, they slowly adapted to this life. They could converse with the Bulgarians because their languages were alike, had tidier huts on the inside, and knew certain crafts they used to spend hours on. With a hammer, a nail, and a piece of iron in place of an anvil, some knew how to turn a silver or nickel coin into a fitted ring with an inscription on it; some knew how to sculpt with their knives and turned plum tree wood into flowered spoons and forks, or into solid cigarette boxes with embossed letters on the lids. Before working here, many used to work the land in the villages and each of them built a small nomadic household and a small heteroclite fortune. One man once showed me his fortune: a deep plate of enameled metal, fifteen wide Macedonian tobacco sheets on a string, a skein of thin wire for sewing buttons, and a pocket barometer that he found on the corpse of a Hungarian soldier on the battlefield.

Every Sunday a weekly market was organized – a kind of exotic bazaar where people could buy clothes or items of urgent necessity, as well as many curiosities. Sitting down on the ground, every prisoner became a merchant for a day, set the item he had for sale on a handkerchief in front of him. Money was rare in the camp – prisoners were mostly trading for objects or services. This type of trade was called *trampa*. The most extraordinary *trampa* I witnessed happened between a Serbian from Moravița and a Frenchman from Upper Normandy. The Serbian offered a small idol sculpted of walnut wood – and received a glass tube from an irrigator in exchange, which he used to build a cigarette. To sell his goods at a higher value, the French swore that the object he had for sale was his most treasured memory of his country...

The Bulgarian commander had a small vegetable garden at the lower end of the camp, where he was working all day long.

One morning, several Serbians had a few tomatoes for sale – new merchandise nobody had had until that moment. Where did they get it? Nobody knew. But the commander found out from the guards. And because there was no other vegetable garden around but his, he felt the need to investigate more closely.

After talking to the Serbians, he continued his investigation in our camp and called me over to him to tell me what this was all about. And again *scrrrr... hîrrr* and *rîcătă* and *kradnătă* – his eyes were bulging. This meant:

"Which of your Romanians sneaked into my garden during the night and stole tomatoes?"

Finally, the investigation stopped at one of our gypsies named Dadu. He had traded the tomatoes to the Serbians for tobacco the night before.

"Where did you get them, gypsy? How come you had them for sale?"

"Well... I found them..."

"Or maybe you stole them."

"May God smite me and send me to hell! May I have no luck if..."

But he couldn't get out of trouble with all his swearing. And the gypsy received a Bulgarian beating that surpassed everything he had ever gotten in his country.

"My brothers, he killed me!" he screamed after escaping and returning to our camp. He was holding his backside with both his hands. "The Bulgarian killed me! The devil take him...."

"Shut up or he's going to hear you..."

"Hear what? He doesn't hear, he doesn't see, he's blind! If he understood when I tried to talk to him, he wouldn't have beaten me so hard for two or three fruits the size of walnuts…"

Life in the camp passed slowly and uneventfully. We constantly heard cannon fire. There was a long chain of bushy mountains towards the south, that started from the Stuma Valley and stretched to Vardar. It was called Belàsiţa. On this peak was installed the heavy artillery, and the deafening cannon blasts especially came from that direction. They were making the air vibrate day and night. Every morning when I woke up I waited for the first cannon blast, hoping that it never came and that peace was close. But days passed one after the other without a change, empty as bubbles of soap.

On a Sunday afternoon, the chirping of a violin was heard from the Serbian huts.

Through unknown circumstances, a Serbian that had worked the fields in a nearby Macedonian village had received this old instrument from a pleased countryman of his, which was very unusual in these parts.

Dadu the gypsy laid face up next to his hut. Hearing the music, he quickly raised his head… Like a hound that caught the scent of prey, he jumped up and started following the sound, sneaking past the sentinel.

Nobody knows for how long he begged the Serbian, but finally he gave him his violin, so he could also play for a bit.

As soon as he held it in his hands, he pinched it a few times excitedly with his long claws, rubbed it with the bow a few times, then he closed his eyes, passionately pressed his cheek to it, and started playing…

The wooden instrument let out a long painful scream, that seemed almost human. A song of mourning, a Romanian *doina*[18] thrilled the air, resounding on these foreign lands for the first time.

---

[18] A traditional Romanian lament song.

The gypsy played with his eyes closed and with his soul far away; large tears were dropping from his lashes, streaking down his copper cheeks that were burned by the heat and dried from so much suffering.

The whole camp slowly surrounded him. Even the Bulgarian guards with their bully of a commander left their tents and stood behind us, listening and trying to see over our heads.

And the fiddler was now playing song after song. He then opened his mouth to voice the pain coming from the violin:

> *Little thread of dry wheat,*
> *You cursed me heavily*
> *When I went to war:*
> *You didn't curse me in the moonlight*
> *So I could die holding my weapon,*
> *You cursed me in the sunlight*
> *So I can dry up under rays*
> *With the Bulgarian at my back...*

Ignoring the ban on entering the Serbian camp, the Romanians came to listen to him as well, after all, it was a song from their homeland. The Bulgarians didn't send them back, and the Serbians didn't stab them.

That's how the reconciliation between the two groups happened.

***

On the evening of that same day, an unusual astronomical event occurred above the Valley of Struma.

As soon as the sun descended behind the mountains of Albania leaving the sky highlighted in ethereal colors, a big ball of fire broke from the sky and fell far away over the Greek territory. That moment must have been witnessed by all the prisoners along the Struma, seeing it glide over the golden twilight silk, slowly as if descending by parachute.

"Mir!" shouted the Serbians, very impressed by the events in the sky.

"Peace, brothers!" replied the Romanians, thrilled by this new sign of hope. "Peace is coming soon…"

"Mir ide s'dîrzo kraşki,"[19] added the Bulgarian commander, pointing his big nose toward the sky.

The heavenly sign either made a mistake or the people didn't interpret it correctly; the peace that everyone gathered there wished for was far away… very far away…

---

[19] Correctly: *Mir ide s'bîrzi kraciki…* Peace approaches quickly…

VIII

The geography I learned in school was insufficient and abstract! Until then, I didn't know you could grow crops twice a year in southern Macedonia... I didn't have many troubles from not knowing this, and I wouldn't continue living in this part of the world even if someone had told me that the spinach grows as big as a house or that you can harvest cucumbers four times a year. Either way, our geography teacher shouldn't have kept this secret to himself when the state pays him to tell students everything he knows.

I saw other curious things around these parts.

In the valley of Struma, I saw rice fields in artificial swamps, just like in the lands of China; to plant and care for this white wheat, which is less nourishing and less tasty than the golden one found on our fields, the poor people had to stand in mud up to their knees all day long – it was disgusting.

On the peak of Belàsiţa, the forests visible from here were actually centuries-old forests of chestnut trees, which had edible fruits. In the valley at the foot of the mountain, there were orchards of fig trees that weren't mentioned in our geography books. And there was more. It was said that on a mountain close by there was a wide field of tea bushes, with hard shiny leaves; the villagers cut them off the branches, and, after boiling them, they rolled them in their palms, supplying all of Bulgaria in this way. It's also said those people earn good money from it, doing nothing else but cutting leaves for the Bulgarians and spitting in their hands.

But Macedonia also has wildlife that's not mentioned in the geography books.

On many nights, we heard strange howls around the camp, sounding as if the cliffs had awoken and started howling at the stars; I couldn't believe it when the Bulgarians told me there were wild jackals that lived here like in the rocky desert of Arabia – until I saw one howling at the moon with my own eyes.

I couldn't say that I had seen lions and tigers. But there used to be lions here a thousand years ago.

Aside from these natural wonders, between the burned stones of the valley lived a species of gray vipers, longer and meaner than the ones in our country. If people weren't thinking about it they could step on their tails. And even if they didn't mean it, they could get bitten and it wouldn't let go until the next day at sunrise. Because of this, our people avoided them like fire. Only the French went looking for them.

One of my French friends told me that nothing is tastier than the vipers in Macedonia, cut in pieces and fried in a pan. He said they were even tastier than hedgehogs, which could only be used for soup… He probably knew about all this because he tried everything so far – simple curiosity he said.

The Italians are picky and more delicate with food: when it comes to small creatures, they only eat their cheese. They don't touch peppers – the Bulgarians invited them to try peppers in vain. However, they ate frogs with every meal, if they happened to find a pond in the area.

There wasn't much that I could do to avoid starving, so I mostly ate fish and biscuits from the Bulgarians. Another man in my place would have given up from the start by eating at least a frog, but I can swear I didn't touch frogs – until later, during the celebrations of Saint Dumitru, when I tasted only one small leg offered by an Italian comrade. It had transparent meat, like jelly, and I was nauseous for three days after; however, they thought it was tasty.

***

Here in Sveti Vrah, where we arrived at the beginning of October, I was lucky enough to meet a Serbian named Braco Iacşiş, the son of a music composer from Belgrade, who offered me his friendship from the first day, and later on, showed me limitless devotion. He was a tall boy, a bit hunched, and sad, with slightly bulging eyes the color of water. The poor boy was taking care of me like he was my mother. Because he was exempted from work for being the leader of the Serbian clan, as soon as everyone else left for work, Branco caught some small fish from under the rocks in the river, which he then fried and served to me for breakfast on a wide fig leaf. I would have eaten gladly, and maybe they would have been enough to satisfy my hunger, if they didn't have so many bones. But Macedonian fish have the most bones in the animal kingdom; from each of its vertebrae poke out small bones sharp as needles, that you have to eat molecule by molecule until your will to live fades away and you feel like throwing them back to the Struma from where they came.

I also became friends with the Bulgarian commander – a sturdy and ruddy lad, with a face brighter and more honest than those of other Bulgarians I've met so far. He had a solid, terrible name: Dilco Țfetcu Savanof ot selo Crușovene okrîc Vracenski.[20] To become acquainted, I gave him a small bottle in which there used to be perfume – he had a lover upstream, in one of the isolated houses where two or three war widows lived.

During the night, when everyone else was asleep, Dilco used to take me on trips along the banks of Struma, both riding one single bulky donkey. A huge white moon from the times of Alexander the Great used to keep us company.

Before reaching his sentimental destination, Dilco would try to explain, which I would mostly understand by his gestures, and to praise the charm and appeal of three indigenous women. Among them was the one he loved. He always tried to convince me to go there with him. But I don't know why I never trusted what he said. I kept thinking that a person eats frogs when he needs to – and believes it's chicken. Aside from that, it was easy to imagine those houses toward which our nocturnal expedition was headed, were already slowly visited by every Bulgarian guard and every German who ended up in the Valley of Struma, being placed far too obviously in the sight of the troops and the line of cannons.

So I would always insist on waiting by the river next to the donkey.

Until he returned, I enjoyed a full hour of peace. The moon was rising higher and higher, appearing to vibrate above the mountains, in the solitude of the sky. It was so bright that if you looked at it for a minute you would feel like sneezing. To find shelter from its almost solar rays, I hid under a silver willow, from where I unmovingly listened to the water flowing and watched the mountains

---

[20] From Crușovene village, Vracenski country (Bulg.).

The moon was rising higher and higher,
appearing to vibrate above the mountains,
in the solitude of the sky

surrounding me. In this atmosphere clear of fog, the outlines of the barren peaks seemed to be cut into slabs of charcoal. Around me, on the ground, everything was white – the road, the rocks, the grass... There was only one black spot on the road downstream, where a cart with oil had spilled the other day.

Sometimes, when you had nothing else to do, you could observe inorganic mimicry in nature... For example the oil and the water. After hiding for millions of years underground, the oil borrowed the color of the darkness under the ground – its natural state, from where it only kept its aspect of liquid soot, wouldn't be seen or guessed by anyone except by the way it smells. The water that was found on the surface imitated the transparency of air and the brightness of the sun; during the night it resembled moonlight...

While my thoughts were turning further away from reality, the donkey next to me was losing patience. It kept nipping at my sleeve like it wanted us to go somewhere together. But where? It shook its head towards Belaşiţa. But that's where the big cannon always broke the silence of the night with its thick barking resembling a sleepy dog, to let us know that nobody could pass through there.

That's when Dilco returned from his lover.

He seemed less lyrical about the charm of his girl than he appeared when he left; he seemed more somber and didn't feel like talking. If I tried to pry it out of him and ask him how things went he would only shrug, pull his cap over his eyes and spit... This also reminded me of the frog. The beauty of the women around here, I thought, was relative and fickle. Now it is, now it isn't.

I didn't have the opportunity to test this belief, until one day when a woman passed through our camp... It was a special event. The people that gathered there from all over the world haven't seen such a thing for an eternity.

This miraculous creature, exotic, and who seemed to come from another planet, stood out mostly because of her clothing. Following the local fashion, she was wearing a sort of coil on her head, made of rolled handkerchiefs. On her feet, she had boots. She was fat with full lips and frowning – it seemed to me that she also had a bit of hair on her chin. If she wore pants when she sat down on the side of the ditch to pull her boots off, you could have sworn she was a Bulgarian soldier in disguise.

Our Romanians watched her unhappily.

"One of these, my brothers, no matter how patient you are, takes away your love for women for life…"

It was true. But not for all of them. The French, however, seemed to be indulgent. Some of their eyes were shining with excitement.

"*Elle est passable*,"[21] one of them dared to voice out, watching her.

I approached my foreign brother-in-arms, the one who spoke this unexpected appreciation:

"For how long have you been a prisoner?"

"For a year," he said with a sigh. "Why are you asking?"

"For no reason. I only wanted to have an idea of how long it would take me to lose my mind if the war continues…"

---

[21] She's ok… (Fr.).

IX

I started to learn Bulgarian.

Helped by Branco and the commander, I managed to pronounce a few difficult sounds from my throat: *crîc*, *ţfic*, which resemble a hiccup more than human speech, and seemed to upset the delicate ears of my teachers greatly.

Both of them were good lads – but what use is it if they don't speak Romanian or at least French? To enrich my vocabulary, I had to point at various objects to find out what they're called.

Curiously, we seemed to get along better, all three of us. There was no thought we couldn't transmit to each other through gestures and grimaces after two or three hours of work. But now that ended. The moment philology came between us, we couldn't understand a thing and we kept arguing.

Branco knew a bit of German aside from his native tongue, which resembled Bulgarian; it seemed he had a German lover when he was younger. I had one as well when I was older than him, but I wasn't capable of learning from her more than I already knew…

Now it's even harder with Bulgarian. The first thing I learned was a traditional song, equivalent to the Romanian *doina*. This is the beginning of it:

> *Malino, mome, Malino,*
> *Ia flenzi mome v'grădnică,*
> *Ia chici ţfete ghiulovo…*

This means: "Malino, girl, Malino – come from the garden – to braid crowns of roses…" Who would have thought? *Capra crapă piatra-n patru*[22] or *fluture pe punte, fluture subt punte*[23] sounds better than *chici țfete* meaning *rose*.

When he saw me laughing at their words, the officer got angry:

"*Zașto ne năuciș coga stradam zarat tebe?*"[24] he shouted at me, red in the face with patriotic fury.

"I'll give you turnips through the fence," I'd reply to him to reconcile with him.

Hearing my reply, Dilco's ear caught words that sounded similar and meant the same thing in his language, and his face would brighten on the spot.

Almost every word in Bulgarian sounds like growling or scratching. *Hand* in their language is called *rîcă*. That's the origin of our Romanian verb *a rîcai* (to scratch) with the nails on the wall. I'm surprised I came out of this alive.

Bulgarians have a few words that are similar to ours – but they have other meanings. The word *mișcă* means *move* in Romanian and *mouse* in Bulgarian. Why? Only God knows.

What was more surprising was that both the Serbians and the Bulgarians made fun of our Romanian language. Before starting to get along with the Romanians, Branco and Dilco only knew the meaning of one word: *mămăligă* (polenta). I don't understand what they found so comical about it…

Now, when they listened to the Romanians speaking, they were especially interested in the termination *-ește* of our verbs and adverbs: *vorbește* (speaks), *oprește* (stops), *popește* (preaches), etc. In truth, after a foreigner notices this termination it starts sounding odd to you and torments you like it was the first time you heard it…

---

[22] The goat cracks the stone in four pieces (Ro.).

[23] Butterfly on the deck, butterfly under the deck (Ro.).

[24] Correctly: Zașto me măciș coga stradam zarat tebe? – Why do I even try when I suffer because of you? (Bulg.).

A word that sounded very amusing to Dilco's ears was *picioare* (feet). Every time he heard it (and he heard it quite often because Romanians liked complaining about their feet hurting to get exempted from work), the Bulgarian would crinkle his nose:

"That's an ugly word! What does it mean in your language?"

I explained to him what it meant. Then I asked him how they say one foot, two feet in the language.

"*Edin krac, dve kracata...*"

That's where patriotism takes them! Dilco had learned in school that Bulgarian is the most beautiful language in the world. That there's no language more harmonious than that – he thought.

Only Branco, the Serbian, had another opinion. When he heard the Bulgarian speaking, he would stay away, smiling. He knew what he knew. He made sure to teach me a Serbian song. The chorus sounded something like this:

> *Hoi! Za trideset*
> *I tri dana,*
> *Nai mon sîrţa*[25]
>
> *Leji rana.*
> *Hoi! Tvoe ruse cose*
> *Drughi da gu mîrse...*[26]

So there was no doubt in my mind, he thought, that Serbian is the most angelic language in the world. It might be related to Bulgarian – but it doesn't have anything to do with it!

---

[25] Correctly: *Na mom sîrţu.*

[26] Oh, for thirty
And three days
My heart is broken.
Oh, your chestnut hair
Another will it up... (Serb.).

Noticing that lyrics make more of an impression on me than prose does, Dilco kept trying to show the beauty of his native tongue through a song. But apparently, he only knew one, which he kept grumbling in a thick voice:

Ot dol ide popişte
Săs dălgoto brădişte,
Şarină gaida pissănă
Săs măniste nizănă...[27]

Unfortunately, I can't reproduce the sounds of this beautiful song...

After so much learning, I couldn't wait to find an opportunity to practice my skills – and prove to myself that I didn't struggle in vain. And that opportunity appeared right then. A chief engineer who supervised the work in that sector, learning of my existence, wanted to meet me and asked to see me on the work site the next day. I wanted to make a good impression so I started the conversation in Bulgarian. With the help of my two friends I wrote down in a notebook and memorized a phrase, through which I wanted to ask: "What important information would you like to communicate to me?"

The next day I showed up, did a military salute, and spoke out without issues the phrase I learned:

"Şto ste turi rîţite u gebuve?"

The engineer looked at me with his mouth wide open. He seemed even more surprised than I had anticipated. Even on the faces of the surrounding people, a pleasant surprise could be read, as they were trying really hard not to laugh.

I had asked him (as I found out later):

"Why are you standing there with your hands in your pockets?"

Realizing I didn't know any more Bulgarian than that, the engineer didn't get upset. He just asked me in French who taught me to speak Bulgarian so

---

[27] Here comes the priest from the valley
    With his bushy beard,
    With his painted bagpipes,
    With colorful beads... (aut. trans.).

well. But I didn't want to tell him. I replied to him that this beautiful language is taught in every secondary school in the country, being a part of the curriculum.

***

The whole time I had spent in those joyful lands until then, I hadn't seen one drop of rain. We started to think that's how the weather was around there.

One night, when we least expected, a storm with big drops of rain started hitting the leaves of our shelters made of braided branches.

In the beginning, still half asleep, we couldn't believe it. Some walked out into the rain to make sure it was indeed storming. After that, this phenomenon didn't seem so unusual anymore; we laid back down ready to fall asleep, glad that we had shelter.

But the rain kept coming down harder; finally, the water started coming in through every crack of the leafy roof, searching for us in the dark, and falling especially on our necks. Nobody knew where to hide, or in what corner to crawl to escape it.

Our camp was in a lower place, between the mouth of Sveti Vrach and the bed of Struma river, with tall hills and slanted plateaus behind us. But who thought that anything like this would happen when we were building our shelters?

After about two hours of heavy rain, when the agitation in the air seemed to calm down, a howl of flowing water suddenly erupted somewhere from the darkness surrounding us. And by the time we realized what was going on, it picked us up – or we went under.

It was a unanimous scream of blended languages, like in the time of the great flood. All the people in the camp stood up as if they were one person. Through the tar-colored night, with water up to their waist, each tried to escape as best they could. Under that divine anger, you couldn't tell who was a Bulgarian and who was a prisoner. By the time you counted to ten, everyone scattered in different directions and filled up the hills behind, looking for safety on higher ground.

The next day, on a Sunday, we were drying our clothes in the sun, looking from up the hill to the valley down below, where our huts used to be. Nothing was left of them – only a few stakes still stuck in the ground here and there, and a few soaked and tattered pieces of roofs. The whole valley was covered in puddles shining in the sun. We had to wait for the waters to retreat, so we could rebuild our destroyed shelters. After the scare of last night, our men couldn't recover from spite and amazement. This was the devil's country! A place that forced you always to have your guard up because you never knew what was going to happen...

The Bulgarians appeared quite upset as well. But they were treating the prisoners nicer than before. The common danger through which we all went seemed to have softened their hearts, sweetening for at least a day the animosity between them and the prisoners.

There was a place above the road, a wide hole from where the sand was dug during workdays; it had been flooded during the night, but the water had drained into the ground leaving a dead drowned mouse behind it.

A guard stopped on the edge of the hole, resting his elbows on his gun. On the other side was a Romanian with his hands behind his back. As they had nothing better to do, they were both looking at the drowned mouse.

"*Mişcă,* "[28] said the Bulgarian in his language, nodding his head in its direction.

"Your mom's moving on ice," replied the bored Romanian. "Can't you see it's dead?"

---

[28] Mişcă = mouse (Bulg.) / it's moving (Ro.).

X

Six people disappeared during the chaos of the previous night.

At first, it was believed they had drowned – and nobody gave them another thought. Soon after that, the Bulgarians realized that the Romanians had run away, after finding some tracks at the edge of the swamp. Aided by darkness, they swam across the Struma, one after the other, while it was raining and the guards were hiding in the shelters. The storm covered most of the tracks they had left behind until the next day at noon.

They were far by now.

Dilco went to the chief engineer to report the news – and didn't come back. A new commander was sent in his stead, who was older and more hateful than the last one. As soon as he entered the camp, he started screaming. He gathered all the guards around him and beat them one by one to enforce his position. Then he sent a few of them to track the runaways and bring them back dead or alive.

For almost two weeks nobody knew the fate of the men who went missing. The guards left in different directions every morning, searched the nearby villages and dug through every valley, hiding spot, and bush, and they came back with a report for the commander:

"Nema!"

***

Meanwhile, lost in the middle of these unknown lands, hunted like animals, tired and hungry, the six fugitives were hiding during the day among cliffs, under river banks, in holes covered by weeds, and during the night they walked straight west, avoiding the villages and commonly-used roads. They walked scattered a few steps from one another, listening for danger. Ahead of them walked Stoica, their corporal, giving way or ordering them to drop to the ground at the smallest sign of danger.

They were young and clever boys, all originating from the mountainside of Olt, Jiu, or Argeş – aside from one boy named Andrei, who was from Dobrogea but his parents were from Ardeal. Brought by the Bulgarians to the valley of Struma, they quickly understood they were fated to die as captives, exhausted from hunger and work, if they didn't find a way to escape. They all slept in the same hut. Following Stoica's advice, they saved up food for weeks from the one that was shared every day. They planned to keep walking west, under Belaşiţa, until they stopped hearing cannons – a sign the battlefield was far away; from there they planned to turn south and cross the border into Greece, which was a neutral country.

Unforeseen impediments stood in their way right from the start. On the eve of their escape, it was hot like summer in the Valley of Struma, but now it was getting colder, and the rain kept coming down and turning into sleet and snow. After walking for three days, they reached the shores of the Strumiţa. They managed to swim across by guessing their way in the dark with the water up to their shoulders, holding onto each other to avoid being swept away downstream. After they pulled themselves up on the other side, they found themselves in a groove covered in snow; their wet clothes froze because of the wind and turned hard like tree bark. The biscuits, their only food, were swollen and mushy. Their flints were good for nothing as well.

They were bitterly discouraged. Curled up in the weeds, they brought their heads together in counsel:

"What are we going to do?"

"We're going to rest here until nightfall... then we keep going," decided Stoica in a harsh tone. Watching everyone with his small green eyes sunken in his skull, with a relentless look like steel, he didn't allow them to oppose him.

"Death awaits us if we turn back either way!"

The others were silent, staring at the ground. Shriveled by cold and wet to their bones, they were thinking again of their homes, toward where their misfortune was carrying them through enemy lands. The sky above was purple.

They planned to keep walking west,
under Belasiţa, until they stopped hearing cannons

The Strumița flowed noisily under the crooked bank. A wet wind hissed in this desolation through the leafless willows of the foreign grove.

After a while, Andrei, the blond and gentle boy, delicate like a girl and frailer than everyone else, started to moan quietly with his face heated by fever and his body shaken by chills. His brothers took him between them to warm him up. Stoica took off his old soaked tunic, drained it of water, and covered the boy with it as if he was a child. And because the boy's teeth were chattering uncontrollably, the leader of the group ended up dressed only in his shirt, clenching his teeth, and sticking closer to his friends.

They walked west for two more days along the desolate Belașița, on rocky paths and foggy wastelands.

They were exhausted and hungry from the journey.

With a gaunt face and dark circles under his eyes, Andrei could barely stand up. The others had to take turns helping him. Todiran helped him the most. He was a native of Gorj, with a hairy face, broad shoulders, and sturdy like a bear, and he always stayed behind to help his sick comrade.

They could hear the cannon fire constantly and the battlefield was not ending…

Becoming more and more unsettled, the leader was searching the dark peak of the mountains with his inquisitive eyes, measuring the distance from the foot of the mountain to the peak, calculating things in his mind…

"We can't keep going forward," he decided during a halt. "We must go through the battlefield… if we could sneak through the French lines we'll escape."

"And what if the Bulgarians catch us?"

His mustache shook nervously, the way it usually did when he felt like someone was against him.

"If they catch us there, they shoot us! We'll die either way. But we'll have tried at least!"

His friends listened to him as always. Stoica had a powerful soul and body, that's why nobody ever dared to oppose him.

So they started walking south and entered the chestnut forest of Belaşiţa. There they stilled their hunger with sweet chestnuts they found fallen among dried leaves on the ground. They rested on soft leaf beds. At sunrise, they started walking uphill again. The forest was dark and deserted. Only howling winds were swaying the top of the trees, slightly drowning the cannon on the peak that could be heard many miles away.

During this time, Andrei, who was overcome by sickness, was barely moving. His face was thin, he was running out of breath, and he was wheezing, probably not even knowing what was going on around him. He was slowly suffocating and leaving drops of blood behind him on the dried leaves.

"Let me die, brothers," he whispered with his eyes closed.

Where could they leave him? They all started walking the same way, and they all had to reach their destination together. Stoica was talking to him constantly, trying to make him forget. Two men at a time would carry him, supporting his arms, quiet, and stubborn.

In the evening, they started hearing voices coming from the peak. While they were slowly and cautiously climbing the slope to the sound of cannons, they suddenly saw the glade on the top of the mountain.

They ended up near the Bulgarian artillery.

All of them stopped in a narrow crevice that was hidden away from view and planned their next move. Andrei dropped limply and voicelessly on the grass. His eyes were glazed over. He wasn't moaning anymore.

Stoica left him with the rest of the men while he went alone to scout the surroundings and spy on the Bulgarians. He was sneaking through the sparse tree trunks, crawling on his belly like a fox... At the edge of the glade, he saw huts and shelters built in the ground on the slope. Behind the heavy artillery, on the curvy road between them, the Bulgarian troops were changing rounds every minute...

That was the moment he realized the gravity of the mission they would be trying to accomplish during the night. How could they pass unnoticed through so many cannons and troops? How could they sneak without a guide through the barbed wire over the infantry line in the valley, without anyone seeing them?

Discouraged for the first time, Stoica went back to his companions. He found them in tears, gathered around Andrei.

"He's dying," one of them whispered, turning his head.

Stoica remained motionless. His whole soul suddenly felt ravaged. He got down on one knee and took his hat off.

At the same moment, they were spotted by a Bulgarian soldier who was watching them with interest from the other side of the vale. Stoica shrugged. He bent over his dying friend and kissed him on the forehead.

A gunshot resounded over their heads, but none of them thought about running.

They were soon surrounded from every direction.

"*Predaite-se* !"[29] shouted a voice.

They saw that none of them made a move, all kneeling and looking down, but none of the Bulgarians could understand what was going on. A few moments later, when they approached them, they finally understood...

They quietly took off their caps and crossed themselves, witnessing the fallen stranger's last breath.

***

The night had fallen. The prisoners were all sitting next to each other on a log in front of a small fire, surrounded by Bulgarian soldiers, slowly chewing some black bread and watching the flames without blinking. The Bulgarians – some

---

[29] Surrender! (Bulg.).

grizzled, others so young they barely had a mustache – were watching them without enmity, somehow seeming glad of this unexpected encounter.

"What are you doing here?" asked an old soldier in Romanian, after watching them with his gray eyes for a while without saying a word. "Where are you coming from?"

"We ran away from the valley of Struma, from the mouth of Sveti Vrach…"

The Bulgarian turned his gaze towards the fire in deep thought…

"If you have gotten caught further away, in the valley, they might have pardoned you. But you're on the front…"

"So what's going to happen to us?"

"You Romanians are in deep trouble… Our colonel has to treat you according to the law…"

The next day, after they slept undisturbed the whole night, the captives were taken to the colonel – a man with a gray beard, calm, and with piercing eyes. He was standing near his hut that was dug in the ground, dressed in a tight coat. A few steps away, a young officer was watching his every move. Lower, in a cluster of fir trees, a troop of armed soldiers was waiting…

The interrogation was short. The old soldier from last night was translating the questions to the captives.

The colonel finally commanded for them to be taken to the shore, with their backs to the troops… But watching them walking away, he had a moment of hesitation. He signaled for them to stop and whispered something to the old soldier.

"Which of you is the leader?" he asked. "Our colonel is asking you: who made you run away? If you tell us, he'll pardon you and shoot him only…"

The captives stopped like in a dream. It looked as if they didn't understand the question. They brought their heads together in counsel.

"Don't say anything, brothers," said Stoica. "I'll surrender... My only request is that if any of you make it out alive, go and tell my mother where and how I died…"

"Are you finished?" asked the Bulgarian.

Stoica, pale, stepped up and spoke in a harsh tone:

"I'm the leader!"

The colonel watched him with interest. He then signaled with his hand to have him taken away…

In the next second, something unexpected happened. The other four rushed in front of their friend:

"He lied! He wanted us to be spared… but he's not the leader!"

The scene unfolded so rapidly, that the colonel couldn't tell what was going on. Then he understood. His harsh soldier eyes and his fiery soul softened with compassion. He turned to his officer and whispered something. He then went to the troop and told them a few words as well, pointing to the five foreign fugitives.

Finally, he approached Stoica and patted him on the shoulder:

"You are all pardoned. Today I will return you to the camp you ran away from. I will see you won't be harmed by your officers."

Our men were sent from post to post downstream along the Strumița and along the mountains, until one day, they reached the small camp near the cursed water of Struma. However, even if the guards were commanded not to harm them, they were punished horribly for all the beatings and the struggles they had to endure because of them.

XI

The railroad in our sector was complete.

A small locomotive was sent one morning – probably the same one that had brought us to the base of the Rhodope Mountains – and stopped near the bridge above our camp and sent a long sharp whistle in the air.

Our job here was done. Now we had to leave these lands and move to unknown places because we didn't have anything else to do here.

On a Friday after St. Dumitru, I said my farewells to Branco and left with a convoy of around two hundred Romanian prisoners, led by the Bulgarians, upstream along the Sveti Vrach river. We had heard that we'd be split into smaller groups and sent to different destinations. I planned to be part of the last group, so I could be sent as far away as possible, hopefully in the mountains; and I chose a group of friends made entirely of young men.

The road curved ahead of us through a wide-open valley. Now the sharp dark peaks of the Rhodope mountains were on my left, to the north; to the south, in the opposite direction was a long row of wooded peaks, from where the cannons of the Aegean Sea sounded further and further away; toward the east, there were more rows of mountains, from where the highest one pointed its barren peak toward the sky from the darkness of the forest growing on its slopes. That one was Pirin-Planina. That was our destination.

Before we reached it, the Bulgarians said we were supposed to halt in a beautiful town called Melnik, where we would receive our bread for lunch. That meant the town was not far away.

The land was spread before us and the whole valley to Pirin-Planina was clear – but there was no town in sight. We could see bright and deserted vineyards on the hills to our right.

"*Cade Melnik?*"[30] I asked the Bulgarians leading the convoy. I was walking beside them so I could see the places better.

"*Tam!*"[31] They answered pointing to a vague spot between us and the mountain, but I couldn't spot it.

A town with roads and churches, no matter how hidden from view it was, couldn't be invisible like a microbe in the air, so much that you couldn't see it even when you were near it. Where could this ghost-town that was on everyone's lips since this morning be hidden?

The water of Sveti Vlah was flowing through the bottom of a deep narrow crack that was dug by the waves in the sand between tall and straight banks. At one point, our path descended between those walls of hardened sand, and we had to walk through the clear river a few times.

Close to noon, we reached a place where other cracks were spreading on the sides of the banks. We stopped under a ravine, on the bottom of one of those cracks in the shade.

"*Tucă Melnik!*"[32] said an old guard pointing to the tall sand wall ahead of us.

If I didn't know Bulgarians to be serious men, I would have thought they were joking. But they don't usually joke. Something had to be hidden behind those steep sand walls...

I got the carriers ready and started walking with them and a few Bulgarians to get our bread from the town, anxious to finally find the answer to this enigma.

After going around a corner we entered another side opening – and found ourselves in the town...

It was hidden in plain sight in a network of deep crevices that replaced streets, with every building being no taller than the level of its surroundings.

---

[30] Where's Melnik? (Bulg.).

[31] There! (Bulg.).

[32] This is Melnik! (Bulg.).

*Meanwhile, our men filled up the bags with bread
for the hungry captives who were waiting for us
near the stream*

The houses had odd architecture. They were built in holes on the vertical wall and looked like caves – only the front of the house with the balcony would be on the outside, supported by tall beams. From those astounding households, the inhabitants had to descend a long narrow stairway right in the street. Very few houses were built on the ground on an actual foundation.

We slipped onto a quiet road and didn't meet anyone at first; however, the shining eyes of women watched us from behind the curtains, but they disappeared quickly into the shadows.

When we reached the official location of military authority – a simple house with four walls, built on the ground – a Bulgarian guard went in with a document for the officer, and the rest of us stayed in the yard, amazed at the hanged palaces around us. No barking, no child's voice disturbed the stillness of this storybook town, which looked as if it had been asleep for centuries between its tall yellow walls. Only a few sparrows were sunbathing on the roof next to us, chirping happily.

After a time, I was invited to go inside. The officer's helper wanted to meet me. He was a bulky and joyful redheaded lad – he was sitting at the table and it was clear he wasn't displeased with the sweet local wines. When he greeted me, his tunic was unbuttoned up to his neck, and he was kind to me, even though it was a bit difficult to understand each other speaking half French and half Bulgarian.

"*Pissatel!*"[33] he joyfully shouted, hitting the table with his fist when he learned I was a writer. "Come here and let me kiss you!"

In the end, he wanted me to remain there in Melnik and to give me a job, but the thought of living alone among strangers in this exotic decorum did not appeal to me at all.

"You *rumanski* are the devil's men..." he tried to explain the sympathy he had for me. "You took the Quadrilateral from us and ate our *cucoșca*[34] in 1913

---

[33] Writer! (Bulg.).

[34] Hen (Bulg.).

when you came to fight with our women. That's all right. You are a lively people with open hearts – I love you too. But these Greek dogs, I would eat fried on coals," he shouts standing up. "They're mean with dark hearts, and they hate us to death, *da ebam maika*!"

He offered me a glass of red wine to toast for the future peace between our countries. When we said our goodbyes, he shook my hand warmer than when he met me.

"Treat the Romanian writer well, or I'll turn you to dust!" he told the guards that were accompanying me.

Meanwhile, our men filled up the bags with bread for the hungry captives who were waiting for us near the stream. The town had only one exit – the one we came through (if you wanted to leave another way, you would have to climb down the cliffs on ladders). On our return, we took another path, so we could arrive in the center of the town. The Greek population pretended not to notice us, even though they all glanced at the bags our men were carrying and swallowed their craving. When we passed a small café with tables outside, a young Greek who was sitting with his head in his palms shouted something sharply in his language without turning his eyes to us. It was obviously a protest against the Bulgarian authority for giving all the bread to prisoners and letting the locals starve...

I stayed behind with a guard after I signaled him to stop at the café. The Bulgarian hesitated for a second – but remembering how the officer's subordinate received me he agreed to sit at one of the tables where we ordered two coffees.

"*Ma scoro, bre!*"[35] he rushed at me to clear his conscience.

The Greeks in the café quickly surrounded me. One spoke Romanian well – he lived in Brăila for four years when he was younger. I found out many interesting things from him – and we kept on talking despite the Bulgarian not understanding anything.

---

[35] Fast! (Bulg.).

"Let's go!" the poor guard shouted at me occasionally, suspecting us of discussing anti-Bulgarian politics in front of him. But to shut him up, I offered him another Turkish coffee, knowing full well that Romanian money had great value around there.

The Greek I was conversing with was not from Melnik. He was from Drama, a town not too far away, toward the south, where he owned a home. Because he was a Venizelist, the Bulgarians had brought him to this place to be "re-educated," so he wouldn't spread any more hostile propaganda at home. Venizelos and his party were part of the Alliance against the Central Powers.

He told me horrible things were happening in Drama. People were dying of hunger on the streets. The Bulgarians were only giving them a handful of corn-meal a week for each person. Whole families were dying of starvation in their homes, burying their dead under the floorboards one by one, so they could receive more food for their dead for a few days. Highborn women had no choice but to sell their bodies to the Bulgarian soldiers for a bit of flour or a slice of dry bread.

While he was telling me all of this, I angrily watched the town square to our left, where right in the middle stood a pyramid of hard sand, tall as a church tower. On its peak, you could see the ruins of old walls...

"What's that thing?" I asked to change the subject.

The Greek man told me there used to be an ancient city there. Over time it kept sliding lower until it ended up on the bottom of these crevices made by water. Because water eroded the sand year by year, it uncovered other walls under the ancient town. It was the skeleton of a prehistoric town, buried by water deposits fifty feet underground – and only a few pyramids were left standing, same as that one, each with its own ruin at the top...

I couldn't help but ask myself, why did the people insist on remaining here for so many years, in a place where nature fancies moving their town vertically either up or down?

For countless generations, its people had lived only from the profit of the vineyards we saw on the low hills on our way here. And maybe the fate of those vineyards was always tied to the existence of artificial caves that were dug into the walls of the town. These caves that had been dug deeper and deeper by locals from generation to generation, with a mole instinct inherited from their ancestors, are only human homes at their openings. Beyond the homes there might be wide cellars, old as catacombs, that spread far underground and ramify, keeping thousands of barrels safe from humidity in their darkness. The noble smell of grape must reveals its whole genealogy when it enters this underground kingdom at the end of autumn, down to any ancient barrel forgotten in darkness, like an Egyptian mummy embalmed with strong substances among other rotten and moldy barrels...

In the end, I found out from the Greek man that during the Roman Empire, the daughter of an emperor had been exiled here in Melnik.

"Which emperor?"

"I don't know. But you can find this information."

"What did the girl do to be exiled here?"

"Oh... is it that difficult to guess?"

I paid, shook the Greek's hand, and left.

It was about time; the guards were looking for us and the men were ready to go.

Soon we got to circle past the corner of the split riverbank, where the only entrance to the town was keeping watch like a tall golden gate – and the town disappeared from view again, with its bizarre architecture and mysterious history hidden in its sandy nest.

***

I cannot remember how long it took to walk from Melnik to the foot of the Pirin mountain.

I was walking among my companions with my thoughts scattered like I was alone. I was thinking about the emperor's daughter who apparently had been thrown into this corner of the world because of a love sin, away from her lover who was thrown into a dungeon or killed at the emperor's command. A long time ago, she wandered these dry lands in the twilight with her loyal servant, watched from a distance by invisible guards, walking with her soul shattered for her lost love. But her footprints have disappeared a long time ago – and the sand on which she walked was washed away.

This melancholic image of the old times awakens other memories in my heart, like shadows of the past projected on the rocky land of Macedonia... Maybe not far from here towered Phillip's palaces, where Aristotle was summoned to tutor a king's son – a prince with a quick mind and a fiery soul who was worthy of his illustrious teacher. The road we were walking on had resounded with the tramping of Bucephalus' hooves, driven by the teenage prince's hand, maybe not knowing that the two of them would later attempt to conquer the universe.

In these lands, at the court of King Archelaus, once came Euripides to live his last years away from Athens. The legend says the misfortunate poet died torn apart by dogs, not far from the Strymon river – which is the Struma river of today... But what curse had brought him there, what disappointments with no cure had caused him to run away from people? He married twice, and was cheated on twenty times, but this misogynist believed in love like no other and brought women the greatest eulogy any poet's imagination could have conjured through his *Alcestis*. Meanwhile, the same great poet mocked the gods and the mortals as much as he could, making them speak aloud during plays things that a man would normally not even think about. But his contemporaries never understood his irony, because the laugh of this *pince-sans-rire* was quiet and did not explode in loud joy like in the comedies of Aristophanes, who only mocked the famous people, not the Man himself or his unchangeable imperfections. That is how Euripides remained in the conscience of future centuries, only as a tragic poet, even though we could say that he was, without his knowledge, the first English humorist – born in the lands of Hellas in antiquity...

Twenty centuries later, another great poet with a somber imagination and sarcastic spirit, walked with his melancholy through these miserable lands, long before death found him in Missolonghi after he wandered all over Europe.

Lorsque le grand Byron allait quitter Ravenne,
Et chercher sur les mers quelque plage lointaine
Où finir en héros son immortel enunui...[36]

These old lyrics that were almost forgotten were resounding in my mind like a whisper from beyond death, conjuring the shadow of my favorite poet during my lonely teenage years, right on the roads where he had once walked...

I then remembered a small episode of his journey through this region.

It is said that the *pasha* of Melnik heard of an English lord who was set to pass by his residence and greeted him at the entrance of the town to offer his hospitality. Lord Byron was walking in front of a small caravan, accompanied by several servants and guides. He was covered in dust like everyone else from his party, and it was hard to make out who he was. However, the *pasha* walked to him without a moment's hesitation and greeted him.

"How did you know that I was the leader of the caravan?" Lord Byron asked through his translator, after exchanging polite greetings.

The Turk unexpectedly replied in French:

"I realized you were a great man because of your small hands and small ears..."[37]

When I awoke from these memories, like from a vivid dream, Pirin-Planina was close. Crowned by shadows, it was towering ahead of us, up to the sky, with its curtain of cliffs and fir trees.

I looked around me. The day was almost over.

I suddenly felt alone among my captive companions, alone with the ancient mountain that was polished in golden twilight up to its peak.

---

[36] When the great Byron decided to leave Ravenna
And to search for some faraway shore on the sea
Where his immortal boredom could end heroically...
(Lettre à Lamartine by A. de Musset).

[37] Je vous ai reconnu pour un grand homme, à la petitesse de vos mains et de vos oreilles...
(Fr.).

XII

The refreshing perfume of early spring welcomed us on the slopes of the foreign mountain, even though it was autumn, and in these times our flowers and weeds withered under the frost. The air was clean, and the sky was deep and blue, but we could feel the humidity of the mountain vegetation like a foggy breeze.

On both sides of the road, young beech shrubbery was bathing its sappy twigs in the sun, ready to sprout again before the old leaves even fell out. Pale eyes of vegetation were showing up in places in these wild thickets, with the grass covered in autumn flowers, looking like a tired flock of small birds with pink and purple feathers. These late flowers that we had in our lands as well during the fall in the forests and orchards had no leaves and no stems and awoke in my heart childhood memories, sweet and sad images, which were even sadder now in the light of the foreign sky.

Our convoy kept getting smaller. By the time we reached the foot of the mountain, we left behind small groups in places picked by a Bulgarian officer. These served as smaller camps. This man was accompanying us from Melnik for this purpose only and was going to stay with us until we reached the highest point with a group of thirty people. Later, I learned the purpose of these small camps that were spread throughout the slopes. Under the command of a road supervisor, each camp's duty was to maintain a portion of the road that was passing over the mountain and tied Eastern Macedonia to the Valley of Struma and the front from Thessaloniki, through Nevrocopol and Melnik.

After a night spent near a Serbian camp, halfway up the slope, that had been there for a while, we woke up at first light and continued our climb.

The narrow white road was curving on the slope through the darkness of the evergreen forests and in some places was revealing itself in the light, looking like a step cut out in the mountain. Looking down I saw an abyss, and above it was a vertical wall of stone. In other spots, the road was narrowed even more by giant cliffs, which the workers before us did not have time to collapse completely. It then continued through more evergreen forests like a slightly curved alley at the entrance of a park, going towards an invisible castle.

We stopped at noon in a large meadow surrounded by birch trees on a smooth slope above the forests. That was meant to be our winter home.

Far in the valley, over the fir trees implanted in the steep slopes, a village was resting between cliffs at the foot of the neighboring mountain. Several homes were spread throughout the valley. The great roaring of cannons from the top of the Pirin mountain would echo over the forests. The men in the lower camps were hearing it from the north.

Behind us and above us there was a thin curtain of fir trees that was separating the men from the bright strip of open field that stretched to the peak. Seen from far away, from Melnik, that bare strip with straight edges looked like a trail left by a razor on a giant's hairy head.

On the first night, we slept around a large fire under the stars. Two young Turkish soldiers, who had been recruited from some part of Bulgaria and armed with old guns, were our only guards. We could have strangled them and run. They knew that much, and that was why as soon as they were left alone with us, they quietly retreated into the shadows and left us alone like they weren't even there.

In the morning, we started to build our shelters. The Bulgarian *feldwebel*[38] had given us an ax and a few iron shovels, which we used to dig our winter shelters on the slope.

But work was going slow. We were expecting a Bulgarian supervisor aside from the two Turks, the one who was to watch over our road work. With him we were expecting our winter supplies. We waited for him like he was an angel from the sky because the mountain air had made us hungry – thankfully, we didn't have to complain about enduring hunger until then. The men went to bed in the evening without having had anything to eat.

---

[38] Sergeant major (Germ.).

*Everyone believed we had been abandoned
there to die of starvation*

We spent the next day in the same way as the previous one, fasting. The men went in different directions throughout the forest, looking for food to no avail. When night came, and we gathered around the fire again, everyone believed we had been abandoned there to die of starvation.

On the third day, it was the same until noon. What were we supposed to do? The Turks did not know any Bulgarian or Romanian. They had been starving like us for three days and were laying on their backs, one next to the other, sighing and dreaming about rivers of milk and mountains of rice. Our men did not even have the strength to curse. That's how weak they were. One of them found some kind of fern with red roots that tasted sweet; boiled in water the suspect-looking weed would leave a sweet juice that could fool the feeling of hunger for fifteen minutes, or even kill you, but not nourish you in any way.

Near our camp, under a ravine, there was a small clear stream where we would go once in a while to drink water on empty bellies. As I had nothing better to do, I started walking upstream to find its spring.

Soon I found myself on the bottom of a gully between two slopes thick with fir trees. There was no path visible and no whiff of wind; a slight smell of rot floated in the air blended with a smell of tree and green fern. Nothing moved around me, only the water was flowing downstream alone, sparkling in the sun, and chirping on the stones.

Bluebells were showing their heads from among the wet ferns. Strips of fresh grass were spreading down from under the trees, which the summer heat helped to grow not long before. But the delicate flower of desolation mostly disappeared, giving its place to less-delicate flowers that just now started to open their fluffy white corollas.

After an hour of walking, I found the spring. It was hidden at the further end of the gully, where the two slopes came together in an arch above a tall clearing. The place was deserted and melancholic. I liked it there. It felt like home.

The stream had its spring in a small basin dug in the cliff, from where the clear water was flowing on the edge of the rock. I could see specks of fine sand on the bottom through the crystal-clear water, and I could see rays of light coming from the heart of the cliff; the water was shivering and curling in silent laughter, like a lover when you touch her breasts. Escaping through the rocks, the small stream was starting downstream gurgling and clinking on its minuscule bed, tolling its sweet small bells through the ferns.

The stream was not lonely, as it had a smaller sibling that was flowing from the right through dry leaves; but you had to stop breathing and listen carefully if you wanted to hear it flowing, as it sounded like a murmur or a whisper.

When I stood up to leave, I was greeted by a wren with its tail spread like a turkey's, that right then came out from a rotted log to see what was going on. Seeing me it started screeching with its beak wide open. Its alarming voice sounded unexpectedly loud in the quietness of that desolate space, and no matter how small it was, it was making an extraordinary scandal for stepping on its domain. It suddenly stopped and the only thing I could hear was the murmur of the spring.

I climbed the slopes with the help of roots and cliffs. I was walking like in a dream, without knowing where I was and without thinking about what path I had to take. I soon reached smoother land between the fir tree forests. The winds from the south were flowing through the top branches with a mysterious and sleepy rustle, reminding me of the long swish of a waterfall.

On a side, between the straight thin trees, I could see a glade in the valley. I came out with a tired pace at the edge of the tall plain, that opened in a bright light of empty meadows covered in juniper.

There were no people anywhere. At the back of a cluster of trees, I found an abandoned wooden cabin. It might have been a shelter for shepherds before the war because there were poles stuck in the ground. They looked like they were left from pens. The ground that might have been flattened by flocks of sheep in the past, was now covered in dwarf grass and pale dandelions.

In a corner of the cabin, under the fallen roof, I found an old pail of wheat. Digging through it I was lucky enough to find a handful of dry grains after a long search. I ate them just as they were, without boiling them, because I didn't have enough for cooking.

From a nearby hill, over the treetops, I was able to spot our camp; seen from here it seemed a lot smaller. I could see some of the men laying in the sun, others pacing slowly as sick insects. It was enough to understand that nothing unusual had happened in my absence.

Hunger is a struggle hard to endure in the first days. The need for food clenches your soul in a single titanic struggle every second. You cannot think about anything else. Slowly the struggle disappears; you start to feel lighter, and your mind is clear and quiet – and you start to realize the danger you are in.

I put my back against the trunk of a young tree at the edge of the forest, which was isolated from its brothers clustered on the ravine; it was standing there in the wind, with its top warmed by the sun. It felt alive next to me, crossed by an intense flow of life from its roots to its top. I had the same stubborn will to live within me, in my body and my hot blood, deeper in my mind than the strange circumstances in which war had thrown me.

If that night we were to sleep hungry again, I thought, if we expected tomorrow to pass in the same way, how many of my companions would be able to stand up and keep walking? Nothing was left for us than to wait for death; or if the Bulgarians sent us food occasionally, we were just supposed to slowly die of starvation and not be able to escape.

What if the provisions they sent from Melnik were stopped on the way? There were so many posts... The temptation was great because bread in these lands was valued higher than gold. You could buy anything with it, including beautiful women from the city.

I had to be quick. That evening I had to find out what was going on.

The Serbian camp where we had slept for a night was only a couple of miles down the slope. The sun was just now starting to set. I had enough time to go there and return by nightfall. It was pointless to wait.

I started almost running down the slope; I cut through the black clusters of trees until I reached the narrow road that I saw from above. From there I could allow myself to think while walking and not be afraid of losing my way.

My plan was ready. If this trip did not bring us any immediate results, we'd start working on solving it during the night... We would tie up the two Turks using their own belts and deposit them at the bottom of the gully, as far away from the road as possible. In one night, we could go to the village and return. There were isolated houses over there, where we could find food for a group of hungry men. Armed with the two old guns from the Turks and disguised with their clothing, two of our bravest men could take hold of one of the villagers, while the others could keep watch in the dark and help if necessary... And then what? If hunger would pull us out of our shelters again, there was another village on the other side of the mountain, toward Nevrocopol; maybe there were more villages, further away...

***

What if during that time a Bulgarian came and asked us about the Turks?

"*Nema Turks*! They ran and left us alone," we would reply calmly and without showing guilt, like a bunch of lambs of God, blaming everything on the fugitives.

The plan was in place and extremely risky. But we did not have a choice. If we did not want to starve to death, we had to do everything in time, using whatever means necessary, because the war wasn't going to last forever.

We didn't go through hell at Turtucaia only to die of hunger. I was meant to die there on the battlefield, so the life that I was still living was a gift from heaven for me, in the same way as a beginner at gambling earns a great sum of money at his first card game. I could risk my life easier than before. I was gambling with my earnings. When death holds you in her claws for too long, even though she loses her grip, in the end, she leaves a stigma in your nature, like the scars from the claws of a tiger that never heal completely. Thus, the taste of danger remains in the soul of the man who had expected to be killed at one point and was forced to kill in turn to stay alive. It doesn't help you later in life if you go on living a normal life after that – on the contrary. On some rare occasions, it makes you superior to others. When you look at the weak-spirited people around you, you have an odd feeling of pride, something found in the psychology of an adventurer who is ready to risk everything on a card, watching the common mortals with irony, as if they were some innocent and disarmed creatures.

When I reached the Serbian camp, the sun was finally setting. Its golden light was polishing the forests on the mountain; that is what happens where there are tall peaks – the sun seems to set in phases.

The leader of the camp was a road lineman, a young Bulgarian with a Slavic appearance, blond, bulky, and with chubby cheeks. He had talked to us before when we had camped here for the night. He had progressive ideas from what I could tell, even though he was not quite a socialist. He followed the ideas of Tolstoy. The lineman had a Serbian acolyte who was short and fat and always had a pipe in his mouth; a factory worker who spewed propaganda during times of peace. I found both sitting at a birch table, eating beans and smoked ham from a big pan.

"Why did you run away from camp?" were his first words.

"I didn't run away, considering I came to another prison camp," I told him in broken Bulgarian.

He knew he was talking to a man who hadn't eaten in three days but didn't even think about offering me a slice of bread. I assumed that was how the followers of Tolstoy were. These humanitarian visionaries only look at the general idea and ignore the details. They see the others in the future. They only see themselves in the present, because they are closer.

Through a Serbian translator, I told him the situation of my camp. I asked him what had happened to our provisions – and if he would allow me to send a letter to the officer in Melnik... Either way, I was addressing him like he was the highest Bulgarian authority by asking him what we were supposed to do to not die of hunger.

He listened to my story smiling sweetly. He then wiped his mouth and replied in his language:

"*Otkradete nekoia ovţà, hozà... otkradete cokto mojite, I eadete!*"[39]

Steal. Steal a sheep or a goat... steal whatever we found and feed ourselves...

---

[39] Correctly: *Otkradnete nekoia ovţà, cozà... Otkradnete colkoto mojette I eadete!* – Steal a sheep, a goat... steal as much as you can and eat!

Okay! Apparently, this was part of his humanitarian doctrines.

Daylight was slowly turning into night when I started back toward our meadow. On my way back, I stopped in a hiding spot in the forest to see if the Bulgarians would send guards behind me to shoot me, using as an excuse that they found me during the night without an escort and that I had run away from the camp.

I was walking slowly, listening to the whispers of the night and the sound of the mysterious forest, listening to the stream flowing in the distance or to the rustling of the wind, even though there was no breeze in the air. The fir trees were standing straight on the sides of the road, letting me spot starlight through their branches, enough to help me guide my steps through the forest, but not enough to betray my presence if I were to hide in the shadows.

Halfway, I heard a man's voice and the beating of hooves; I hid behind a tree trunk and remained motionless. The voice came from close ahead of me. Then I heard him further away because the road was turning toward a narrow hollow in the cliffs; then it got closer again... There were two men: one on horseback and the other one on foot. They were speaking loudly in Bulgarian. They passed me without noticing I was there. Only the horse turned its head slightly in my direction and huffed to let me know it saw me.

***

When I reached the birch forest, the sweet smell of steak greeted me from afar. I could not believe it. I quickened my steps to see what had happened...

There was a great feast around the fire.

Without waiting for the Bulgarian to allow them, our men had stolen a goat from a flock on the mountain. They were now eating it like a group of cannibals, near the fire that was casting its light on the dark edge of the forest, sharing big pieces of meat among themselves, cooked at the stake without bread or salt.

They kept a very big piece for me as well, which I fried on the spot above the giant pile of embers.

Then they told me how it all happened.

*Our men had stolen a goat. They were now
eating it like a group of cannibals*

They heard the sound of a bell in the evening coming from the valley. Four men sneaked down the slope like a pack of hungry wolves and found the flock under a ravine. When they found an opportunity, Toader Coban grabbed a goat by the leg, pulled it, and flattened it to the ground in the junipers; Gheorghe Andronic held its snout in his hands to quiet it, and Lazăr Ilie Drişcă bled it. They waited for nightfall to drag it uphill, which was exhausting considering they were starving. That was it.

"And the Turks?"

"I gave them each a piece and they were very thankful."

Truthfully, I could see both of them in the dark, sitting away from the rest of the group, watching the fire and chewing slowly. They did not seem at all upset.

"What did you do with the hide and the horns?"

"We threw it there in the forest with the head..."

This was not good. The owner of the flock could find it if he went the next day looking for it. Seeing all the signs, he would understand it was a man who had done it, not a beast.

There was a species of pine growing there called bora, which had a pleasantly smelling sap. If you lit up a twig, it would burn slowly like a torch, without being extinguished by the wind.

We took a few bora twigs from my provisions, lit one up, and entered the forest with Lazăr Ilie Drişcă to look for what was left of the goat.

To remember where he had thrown it, he was walking ahead; I was following close behind guiding myself by the rustling made by his steps, keeping the light low towards the ground.

On the yellow carpet of pine needles, I was casting light on damp foliage, shining on emerald-colored ferns, black shiny roots curled up like long snakes under the ground. In spots, I could see overturned stumps, and at every step, there were motionless gray trunks, that were appearing like ghosts around me and were disappearing in the dark as I was walking away.

"Let's turn to the right," the man ahead of me whispered, but I couldn't see him.

At that moment, I noticed a sort of gnarled stump a few steps away, next to a tall leaf... I turned the fire towards it and backed off. It laid there on its neck, with its horns pointing to the ground, showing its teeth, with its snout pointing up. It even had a small beard. It was looking at me through its eyelids, like a devil's head coming from under the ground in the light of my fire, ready to start bleating happily.

When we returned to our camp where the fire was still burning, everyone was belly-up asleep in the heat of it, nestled on a rough bedding of pine needles. Only one of those poor men who had been crawling around like maggots from how starved they had been, was now sitting up with his arms around his knees, watching the fire. The rustling of our steps on the grass made him turn his hairy cheek towards us, illuminated by firelight.

"What were you thinking about?"

"Not much. I was just sitting here thinking what a good thing it would have been if after this goat we were given a woman as well..."

XIII

Our hideouts on Pirin-Planina, which we dug in the slope, resembled the opening of a tunnel pointed toward the heart of the mountain. And they did not resemble in any way the flimsy huts in the valley of Struma, where we slept on the ground and counted the stars through the roof. Here we even had doors at the entrance and a rudimentary chimney to let the smoke out when we had a fire burning. On the ground, we laid a thick carpet of leaves, and in the corner, we had a pile of soft evergreens each, so we slept on soft bedding and had sweet dreams smelling of sap. There were no windows: daylight entered through the door, even though it stayed closed most of the time. When we wanted to smoke our home, we lit up a small bora branch – so we did not need myrrh, incense, or Armenian sheets. After extinguishing the fire, I had a small night light in my shelter to scare away the evil spirits. I had bought a few chestnuts from a Serbian who got them for cheap from a local. I kept them for a few days in melted sheep tallow; if you made a hole in one of those and stuck a few threads of cotton in it, you could have a candle that lasted all night...

That's how things were in times of war. It stops time and rolls back everything on earth, turning into living icons in every stage of human civilization. In the big cities, in the distant metropolis, electric lights were still shining on the streets and in the comfortable homes, rarely darkened during alarms. On the other side, near the front, we were living underground like people lived thousands of years ago, eating only goat meat, and waiting for humanity to discover agriculture. Below us, other men were lurking in the darkness, ready to jump out at the first sign and kill each other like beasts.

For whose divine eyes was this entire spectacle taking place?... Maybe one of the children of the great Unknown, reaching the learning age and being a bit slow, wasn't able to learn the long history of humankind, except through this intuitive method. In the teachers' opinion, there was no better way of learning for children; only a mature person would be unable to use this method...

A bizarre metaphysical spirit that was also superstitious, could ask himself less ironic questions. Why did the great misanthrope choose to ink some lines and not others on the map of civilization? Why did his brush, dampened in the ink of prehistory, line such and such area, leaving the rest white? And why did he choose us and not others to return to the Stone Age?

A man can think about many odd things while resting underground during the night, looking at a chestnut on fire...

But thoughts don't have meaning anymore. I was to wait there as in a dream, like the wheat waits for the spring in the ground; then I would leave the dark-ness, see the sun again, and feel the sweet joy of life, like I was born again. Until then, I had no other choice other than to take part in the unfolding of this tumultuous dream that I was living, like a man who dreams while in a deep sleep but realizes later on that it had been only a dream.

***

They sent a supervisor who spoke Romanian well. He was still young, and dressed in a military uniform. His name was Stan Ion Boldişcu, and he said he was Romanian, originating from the Dolna village near Vraţa. He wasn't both-ering us much; he only took a group of people every day to check the road and repair it if there was any damage. With him came the Bulgarian with our sup-plies. He left a few loaves of black bread for us, a few onions, and a few pota-toes, after which we stopped seeing him. Our men looked at those official pro-visions with suspicion: they knew what they knew... If we were to rely on the Bulgarian crops, we would have died ten times already. Luckily, the goat of that night was followed by a sheep, then by another goat, and so on, either sheep or goats. Every three-four days we had fresh meat stored in one of the shelters.

We informed Stan Boldişcu of our habits right from the start, and he was not surprised. He even joined a few of our men to a village from where they returned with two chickens and with a big wheel of tobacco leaves on a string... Why would he be surprised? Toader Coban and Lazăr Ilie Drişca turned out to be extremely skillful at this type of work. They might have not been very godly before the war. Who could know what others did before the war?

The supervisor seemed to be an honest man. He swore he had never stolen anything in his life – before the war. I started improving my Bulgarian from him and enriched my vocabulary. He was a good man and friendly, but much too talkative and loved women more than anyone I've seen. When he talked about the women in his village, he would lick his lips. His goose eyes, blue and washed like the eyes of a lascivious woman, would shrink and dampen with pleasure when he spoke about his love adventures... how he had walked on the village road during a holiday with a friend, holding him by his waist and singing *Ot dol ide popişte*[40] and other great songs, and all the wives had come to the windows to see them because all the girls were fancying them. If you think about it, he was a great nuisance!

***

The days passed by. I started getting used to this free life of an outlaw. Every day I felt healthier and stronger after the hardships I have endured. On some mornings, I would wash in the icy waters of the stream, in a hole I dug and lined with stones and grass. I used to run wet to my shelter, so I could dress up in the heat inside. Instead of coffee with milk, I had a piece of well-done meat, still sizzling in its own juice. After that, if I felt like it, I'd go with Stan Boldişcu to work on the road. With a heavy hammer and an iron chisel, we made holes in cliffs that were sticking out too much. We filled the holes with gunpowder, stuck a wick in it, and set it on fire, then we'd run to hide behind a corner where we waited excitedly for the roar of the explosion, which sent echoes through the valley. It was like a party for us. After that, we used to lift heavy boulders and throw them in the ravine to see them rolling down the slope like some rams; one by one, if you knew how to set it on the edge, they'd speed up and could roll for half a mile down the slope, destroying everything in their path.

On other days, I remained in my shelter. With the tip of my knife, I carved braided letters in the lid of a big cigarette box made of plum tree wood, a craft I had learned from the Serbians; or I cut tobacco leaves on a log, organized

---

[40] The priest is coming from the valley (Bulg.).

them by color and made my provisions of three kinds: Macedonian tobacco, yellow and soft like silk, coppery tobacco, and strong black tobacco.

***

But everything comes to an end.

The first sign for me that this patriarchal life was ending and troubles were on the horizon, coincided with the first signs of winter, which in these lands resembles autumn.

During a foggy evening, Lazăr Ilie Drişcă returned from his usual expedition scared and panting with effort:

"The Macedonian caught me! He's coming behind me..."

"How did he catch you? Where?"

We all gathered around him.

"I'll tell you in a second... Give me some water first!"

From his rushed story, I managed to reconstruct the scene:

Using the milky darkness of fog, Drişcă approached the flock that was walking downhill and grabbed a sheep. He pulled it backward, not far, in a hole. While he was leaning over it to pull out its insides, he saw a giant shepherd, as big as a bear, who stopped three paces away in the fog, trying to see what the man was doing crouching on the ground. Drişcă did not lose his cool. Before the other man saw what was going on, he lifted the sheep by its legs, spun it in the air, and hit him in the head with it. He then abandoned it and ran.

That was a stupid thing to do!

Before he finished his tale, there came the shepherd – carrying the sheep and with a bloody cheek, roaring and cursing in his language, and we thought it would never end. Boldişcu tried to talk to him calmly, invited him by the fire, told him nobody had been away from the camp at that hour, that all sorts of suspicious people frequent the mountain – and he told him various other things to calm him down. I joined them, offered him a cigarette, and tried to make him sell us at least a part of his sheep for cash, so we could have a taste of sheep from Pirin-Planina. In the end, we made peace with him – and he left.

A few days later, on a Sunday morning, a group of dark people showed up on the other end of the meadow, walking up to our shelters silently.

Their demeanor seemed odd to me. What were they doing there, where nobody passes through? They were coming toward us and seemed to have a well-defined plan in mind because they were not talking among themselves...

Stan Boldişcu was not there. He had left the evening before for one of his lovers. I called the men out of their shelters and shouted for the ones who were nearby with their business. We all stood up in a single row, waiting for the events to unfold.

Meanwhile, the strangers were getting closer. I counted them. There were fifteen men armed with clubs and bats. We were twice as many but unarmed; only a few men grabbed a piece of wood or a shovel, while Lazăr Ilie Drişca hid the ax behind his back...

The two Turks understood what was going on and were watching these preparations with excitement. The warrior spirit of this nation suddenly awoke in them. When we least expected it, these men who were so mellow before, jumped in front of us with their guns ready and pointed toward the enemy. One of them shouted:

"*Nazat!*"

And the strangers stopped ten paces away. The moment was critical. The troops were standing face to face, examining each other and frowning, ready to start the battle to the death. I was not thinking about anything else, only that whatever the result of this fight would be, only misfortune awaited us from now on.

In that tense moment, a long yell resounded from the other side of the meadow. Everyone turned their heads. It was the voice of Stan Ion Boldişcu, who was running towards us, waving his arms, and asking for an armistice.

When he reached us, we started a discussion.

The Macedonians accused us of theft. They complained we stole from their flocks and asked to search our shelters to look for proof of our plunders. Boldişcu told them that was not possible – *ne moje*. He told them this was a prison camp, and the prisoners are used as army troops. Those who got into the camp without written approval from the officer in charge had to be held accountable in front of the army. Soldiers did not find anything funny during the war... So, with good words or with threats, they were appeased. In the end, their leader spat to the side frustrated. He signaled his friends to follow him – and they left. They walked down in a line back where they came from.

As soon as they were out of sight, Boldişcu started laughing. The others joined him. Only the two Turks quietly retreated and sat on the ground with their eyes closed – they went back to being the same people as before. But our men began to see them in a new light...

Thus, our life started being a lot harder. The owners of the flocks knew who had taken their animals. They counseled each other and set guards. There would be no way for us to steal anything, maybe just rarely and it would be dangerous. The problem of food threatened our lives again.

The uncertainty of the following day kept growing and it was blending in with the fine rain that kept coming increasingly often, like a gray veil over the valley. The forest around our meadow was gloomy and quiet. The empty trunks were wet and not a breeze could be felt.

We were going out in the morning to listen for the great cannon and look at the waves of dark vegetation with our hearts clenched by sadness and unrest.

The fog from the valleys would sometimes lift toward us and cover the top of the trees in the meadow. Through its white darkness, we could not see anything. A strange, supernatural silence surrounded us from every direction and made us speak in hushed tones; even the sound of our voices seemed to come from far away, from the ground. The charm then disappeared; the fog slowly lifted – all that was left were the waves of darkness on the slopes of the mountains.

It snowed two times. We all left our shelters to see the miracle. The motionless fir trees on the edge were barely visible through the curtain of snow. The big white snowflakes that touched the ground didn't have the strength to fight against the blades of grass, which would defy them, grab them from the air, and turn them into drops of dew. The meadow remained green.

In an afternoon, I spotted a Bulgarian soldier coming uphill from the direction of Nevrocopol, with a bag on his shoulder and with his coat around his waist. I walked downstream and greeted him. When he saw me, he was very surprised. He didn't know from where I showed up in the middle of the forest.

I offered him a cigarette and invited him to sit with me on a rock to rest. He was going to Melnik. From his tale, I understood that he was looking for men from the prison camps that worked on the railway, so he could send them to Sofia...

The whirlwind I was living in had taught me not to pass up good opportunities.

I tore a page out of my notebook, on which I wrote a few words in French. I gave the Bulgarian my cigarette box and asked him to take my note to the officer's acolyte in Melnik, and that I was friends with him

A few days later, a young Bulgarian guard stopped in our camp, tired and sweaty from climbing; he pulled a *răspică*[41] from his hat and asked for me... My friend from Melnik fulfilled my request: I had been signed up at my own request to become a railway mechanic.

On that day, I left the Pirin-Planina camp forever, determined to confront the unexpected and hostile circumstances with which I still had to fight.

I left for Sofia to meet my locomotive.

---

[41] Paper (Bulg.).

XIV

As soon as we left the camp and the stone road, we turned left to go straight through the forest.

Dimiter, my companion, knew hidden paths through the valley that would take us to the same destination, the west side of the Pirin mountain. The path downhill had many turns and detours, which were good for loaded convoys, but not that good for people in a rush like us.

We were walking through dangerous abyssal places without talking; we would just sometimes sneak a look at one another. The Bulgarian was a nice, joyful guy, with his old cap sprightly pulled on one side. Because we were alone through those lands, and he couldn't be sure what type of person he had as a companion, he kept his bayonet close. We then started talking and we became friends. He said he had received orders to take me to a certain place in the valley of Struma by the following evening, from where I and other prisoners would be taken to Sofia.

We were lucky to have great weather. Purple spring clouds were floating in the sky, split into small parts by the mountain winds. The sun was coming in and out of the clouds. When it was getting blocked by a cloud, the forest would suddenly become dark as night; as soon as the cloud passed, bright sun rays shot through the black peaks, casting golden lights on the dry leaves that were sparkling like jewels.

The path we reached was running downhill through the forest, cutting through narrow clearings and slopes, reaching hidden gullies with small streams on their bottoms.

I was starting to get hungry. I thought the Bulgarian had a slice of bread in his bag, a dry onion, and other goods. I had nothing. I had been afraid to take the goat steak with me when I left, to avoid letting the Bulgarian notice my comrades' habits that I was leaving behind. I felt a twinge of regret. Dimiter told me, without me asking about it, that he was hungry as well, and he didn't really have anything with him. He laughed, showing his white teeth from under his mustache, which looked like the fangs of a young wolf ready to bite. I was thinking about how hard it was to live in this wilderness – you could die of hunger with money in your pocket because there was nothing to buy. In the city, it would be different. I was glad to have enough silver coins for better days, as I did not have what to spend them on.

While I was deep in my thoughts, I noticed a man ahead of us, near a clearing... He was climbing slowly toward us, pulling a donkey by the bridle behind him.

The Macedonian had not seen us yet. Dimiter put a hand on my shoulder and remained motionless, with his sharp eyes watching carefully. He then started walking again and talking loudly, with the demise of a placid and carefree traveler.

"*Dobru den, gospodin,*"[42] he greeted the stranger that was getting closer.

But a few moments later, the man turned around sharply and shouted:

"*Stoi!*"[43]

We took him between us. The man quickly grabbed his knife, but the Bulgarian's bayonet was faster and already pointing at his chest... He turned his eyes to the right, then to the left without moving his head. The place was wild and desolate. Aside from this, we were two, and he was one; and the ravine was close...

"*Tirsi!*"[44] shouted Dimiter without taking his eyes off him.

I searched the packsaddle on the mule. I pulled a big loaf of bread, enough to feed three people. From the other side, I pulled a wooden jug, secured with belts; it was full. I did not really know what I was supposed to do with it.

---

[42] Good day, sir! (Bulg.).

[43] Wait!

[44] Search him! (Bulg.).

*Dimiter then walked away from him
with his gun pointing at his chest*

"Zemi ciotra!" ordered me the Bulgarian. "Take the jug as well."

The stranger watched us grimly, from under his bushy eyebrows, without saying a word. I heard him sighing. To make things fair, I threw him a five lei coin.

Dimiter then walked away from him with his gun pointing at his chest. We left him there and kept on walking.

We were now walking downhill with quick steps, looking behind us often. My companion stopped from time to time, listening carefully – but there was no noise behind us. All we could hear was the wind blowing through the pine trees. The surrounding forest remained calm. After half an hour, we suddenly stopped in a small clearing – because we were both impatient.

The Macedonian's brandy proved to be extremely strong. By the time we finished our meal, the forest was spinning around us.

We then walked down the last slopes of the Pirin mountain, lively and nimble, like the entire world was ours. Dimiter held me at the waist and dragged his gun behind him, singing loudly:

> *Tri meseța v' Gorna-Bania*
> *I cetfirta văf Sofi-i -i-i-a...*[45]

I can't remember the places we passed through or how we reached Melnik at sunset.

***

We didn't enter the city. We passed by its gate and went around, through a lower side crack of the sandy hills.

My thought was that we would stay in town for the night, at the military house, from where we would leave the next day. My companion, however, had another idea. He had a better plan, which he didn't want to share with me.

---

[45] Three months at Gorna-Bania

The forth at Sofia... (Bulg.).

He guided me under the tall sandbanks, to a much darker place; he left me there in a sandy hollow, letting me keep the bread and the brandy, as we had more than half of each. And he told me:

"*Ciacă tucă, rumanski...*"[46]

He was going to town without me, probably to bring me something good for the night.

"*Ma scoro, bre!*" I shouted back to him, knowing Bulgarian quite well at this point.

I understood nobody had to see me there in his absence.

The cold mountain air and the tiredness from the journey caused me to be almost sober. I laid down face up in the sand, looking at the stars. I didn't feel any movement in the darkness: the Sveti Vlah River was flowing without a murmur a hundred steps below, and far away I could hear the screeching of wheels against the gravel in the dark.

After waiting for about an hour, I heard light steps coming from the direction of the water. I lifted my head... Three shadows were quietly walking through the dark, whispering.

"*Rumanski,*" whispered Dimiter

He came from the town accompanied by two young Greek girls.

When I stood up, my companion grabbed one of them and pulled her toward him in the shadows, after which he pushed the other girl into my arms, who was thin and light as a feather...

We dined under the stars, all four of us sitting in the sand. Dimiter even brought a piece of cheese from the town. The girls ate greedily from our bread – however, they did not want to touch the brandy.

The one next to me was named Caliopi, and she only spoke Greek. I told her in her old mother's tongue, the beginning of the history of Xenophon.

---

[46] Correctly: *Ciacai tuka, rumanski...* Wait here, Romanian... (Bulg.).

"*Mitros te ke patros ke ton alon progònon apanton...*"[47]

And I added in modern Greek the only words I knew, from a poem of Byron's"

"*Zoi mu, sas agapo...*"[48]

Before sunrise, the girls asked to go home. They were afraid of being seen in daylight. We said goodbye to them and to love after we accompanied them to the town gate. We returned to rest in the same spot, where we believed our sleep would be sweeter than in any other place.

When we woke up in the morning, the sun was already up, and I had the feeling everything had been just a dream. But there were still footprints in the sand around us...

***

On the same day, we reached the waters of the Struma and Dimiter gave me away with my papers to the officer who was leading the group of prisoners to Sofia.

Before he departed, my friend with whom I had shared good and troubled times, shook my hand and whispered:

"*Sbogum, moi brate! I mnogo zdrave!...*"[49]

He might have hugged me if the others had not been watching us... In the two days since we met, we had done many exploits together. We had robbed a man in plain daylight, had gotten drunk, and had corrupted two girls. It wasn't a small deal.

---

[47] Of mothers and fathers and all the other ancestors.... (Greek).

[48] My life, I love you... (Greek).

[49] Farewell, brother! And I wish you health!...

XV

The group of foreign comrades I joined, was waiting on the side of the railroad to climb into the open wagons of the train, during the night or the next morning. The Decauville train passed through here twice a day going toward Radomir.

It was a colorful mix of odd clothing, from which the idea of uniform had disappeared: a whole collection of ethnic types of all kinds – Russians, French, Italians, and a lot of Serbians – speaking as many languages. There were no Romanians however. Or, if there were any, it was hard for me to find them at first glance because there were so many people.

Some slept on the ground, with their heads against their luggage; others were busy around an improvised fire, or speaking among themselves, sitting on the bank and throwing stones in the water of the Struma to pass the time.

To find someone to talk to, I climbed on a boulder and shouted over their heads:

"Hey! Which one of you is Romanian?"

Then one of the men who was laying down face up lifted his head and replied to me from the other end of the group.

"Here! I'm Romanian!"

I walked to him. He was a bulky Christian with a mustache, originating from the land of Tutova. His name was Dumitrache Nedelcu. We walked away from the rest to speak privately and each of us smoked a cigarette from my strong tobacco brought from Pirin.

"Did you work on the railroads?" I asked him

"Yes, sir," he replied a bit harshly. "I was a mechanic."

"A mechanic you say?"

"Well…"

I had not expected that. I looked at his face and I felt like laughing.

"What did you do there?" he asked me, more restless than vexed. "You were a mechanic as well?"

"Not really. But I became one a week ago... I guess two mechanics were fated to meet in the Bulgarian country."

Dumitrache was looking at me not knowing what to believe. He was probably glad to find a friend to talk to, but he didn't trust me. Maybe I was a Bulgarian spy – you could never be sure.

"And what part of the country are you from?"

"From Moldavia," I replied to him vaguely.

"Really? I guess it's a good thing we met."

"Yes, yes, a great advantage."

Dumitrache was silent for a while, deep in thought.

"Sir, I'd really like you to tell me… what do you think the Bulgarians want from us when we reach Sofia?"

"What do you mean? They're going to give us each a locomotive."

"Yes, I know that... But don't you think they're going to ask one of their men that's skilled in this, to show us something in the beginning, how to operate it? To tell you the truth, I forgot my way with the screws, since I didn't touch them for such a long time."

"You shouldn't hope for that," I discouraged him. "They won't show you anything. They'll put you in the locomotive and that's it: go, boy! Don't you know how Bulgarians are?"

When he heard me talking like that, Nedelcu became upset. He set his eyes on the ground and sighed from the bottom of his heart without saying another word.

"Dumitrache, it seems to me that you are not actually a mechanic like you told me."

He swallowed and hesitated.

You must be there and see with your own eyes
if you want to learn

"I'm not," he finally told me with some difficulty. "In truth, I didn't go far and didn't do much. But what was I supposed to do? I didn't want to starve in that rocky country..."

"Who signed you up?"

"An officer from the mouth of Strumiţa."

To calm him down a bit, I showed him there were ways in which he could get away with it. I taught him that once he found himself in Sofia to tell them he was actually a brakeman and the officer put him down as a mechanic by mistake.

But he was set on becoming a mechanic.

"It wouldn't be a bad idea to speak with the Italians over there and find out from them how things are done on the locomotive. You know, pieces of information here and there – maybe you can steal some craft and tell me some after that."

"It's pointless, man, you can't learn how to be a mechanic just from words like you believe. You must be there and see with your own eyes if you want to learn."

"Mark my words, we're going to be in deep trouble," he said. "The locomotive is the devil's machine, not a toy. If you don't know all its tricks, you can damage it. When you want it to go forward, it goes backward... And throws you in a ravine with wagons and all. Or, if you touch it where you are not supposed to, it will start squealing like 70 sows together and wakes up a whole city. What are you going to do then?"

The following morning, we finally started our journey.

In the second wagon from the rear, where we had ended up, Dumitrache Nedelcu was sitting nervously next to me. At every stop, he got down first to look around the locomotive. When we departed again, he was the last one to climb back on. He was silent, preoccupied, and frowning all the time.

"One thing that really bothers me," he finally said, "is that I can't be there in the front when they start it and turn it off, to observe what they do... I know everything else. I saw how they feed it coal and water, I saw how they oil its joints. I couldn't see what they did under it because the Bulgarian wouldn't let me."

"Which Bulgarian?"

"The one running the locomotive. He doesn't like me getting too close, he knows I'm trying to learn the craft. What a mechanic... He's all smudged with coal, you can only see his eyes. He has big white eyes, like two French coins. As soon as he sees me getting close, he stares at me and threatens me with the whisk."

"What whisk?"

"You don't even know what that is? You're going to have a hard time when they give you your own locomotive... It's a long iron rod with a wet rag on one end. You wet the coal with it when you want to make it sizzle and burn hotter. Every locksmith or blacksmith has one, and so does a mechanic. What would happen on the road if you didn't have it? Look, this Bulgarian, however small he is, has a long whisk."

The train often stopped because the distance between stations was too small to fit the size of the locomotive. After one stop, Dumitrache sat next to me sulking and said:

"He was about to burn me. He sprayed hot steam on my nose."

At the following stop, my friend returned earlier than expected. He was rubbing the back of his neck.

"What happened, Dumitrache?"

"I can't learn anymore. The officers noticed me... As soon as the train stops, they all watch me. As soon as I walk toward the locomotive, they chase me from every direction and punch the back of my neck. The only thing I have to work with is what I learned so far..."

***

We were moved to another train in Radomir. That one was bigger, and nobody was allowed to get down anymore.

When we reached Sofia, an engineer in a military uniform came to search for us using a list.

"Mechanic?" he asked in Bulgarian when he reached me.

"No, I'm not a mechanic," I replied in French.

"You couldn't be one," he said. "If you were a railroad mechanic, your country wouldn't have sent you to war... But on the list, I can see you recommended yourself as a mechanic. You lied. Why?"

"So, I could come to the city. Otherwise, I would have starved in the mountains of Macedonia..."

"Are you aware that you could be shot for this?"

"Better than starving to death..."

The Bulgarian thought for a few moments. He didn't know what to do with me. Finally, he turned toward a guard who was waiting with his bayonet ready.

"Take him to the train station in Nadeja, to the wagons," he commanded him without looking at me.

The soldier took me immediately:

"*Haida!*"

As I walked by, I saw Dumitrache Nedelcu who was waiting his turn. He had heard me talking and now saw me being led away by the sentinel, but he didn't know what would happen to me.

"Sir, it's my turn soon. I can't speak Bulgarian... What am I supposed to do?"

"Don't be afraid! Tell them you were a brakeman like I taught you. Do you understand?"

"*Haida, bre!*" grumbled the soldier, pushing me from behind.

So, I started walking with the guard behind me through the sleet.

XVI

What possessed me to leave Pirin-Planina?

Isolated on the peak of the mountain we could have died of hunger in the wilderness, but at least we had a mild climate and clean grass under our feet – it wasn't cold, there was no sleet, there was no mud up to my knees like in this sinister place, called Nadeja, where we ended up.

That's what happens when a man has too much good in his life and wants more.

In southern Macedonia, away from the prying eyes of those in power, more nations were living together, Bulgarians, Romanians, Serbians, and French, almost all of them young, with their souls still clean despite the hardships, at peace with the life that the war gave them, and getting along with each other, sometimes even building friendships with their former enemies.

Here, it was clear I entered civilization, that I was close to the capital of the country. The hate Bulgarians felt toward us, fueled by the newspapers, has not been stilled yet. In these places, I found the regime of the first days of my captivity – the same enmity as in the beginning; the Romanian prisoners from this damned camp were living a hard life of convicts, removed from the protection of any law... No, this time I cannot, I don't want to, and I must not write metaphors. I'll simply show you the facts, just as I've seen them.

The Nadeja train station was a big hovel of timber, placed in a field a few miles away from the city. On the field around it, under a gray sky, the Romanian prisoners were working from dawn to dusk under German leadership, guarded by Bulgarian soldiers, working on various parts of the railway – bridges, lines, and embankments. During the night they slept huddled next to each other (three hundred and fifteen people when I arrived there) in seven wagons meant to carry cattle or goods that had been abandoned on a closed railway line, away from the others.

Around the wagons, there was sticky mud packed from traffic. Next to the wagons, above a hole, a slanted shingle roof sustained by two poles on one side, was used as a kitchen area.

We had to carry water in buckets from a mile away, from the yard of a military barrack – and that was only enough for the kitchen. The men never washed; they drank water from a ditch or ate snow from the field.

Our poor peasants didn't have anything left of their humanity. Dressed in dark rags, you couldn't even identify that the wet wind or the sharp winter wind was blowing in every direction, with rags tied with twine wrapped around their feet, skinny, dirty, with burned skin, glassy eyes, with their minds lost from so much misery. They all looked like corpses that crawled out of the ground and walked into daylight dressed in their funeral clothes.

As they returned from work, they pushed each other, cursed each other, and shouted in ragged voices. Each would pull out a broken plate or a tin can they had found on the side of the road, to receive a bit of bean broth they drank in a heartbeat. Others would bend over big shared pots and eat from them like dogs. They never had any bread for dinner. They always ate all of it in the morning. Many of them only received a quarter of a loaf; the rest was kept by the officer to trade for tobacco – because the head of the guards would sell them tobacco, dealing for bread a few days prior, which he would later sell in the city for a good price.

At nightfall, the men were locked in the wagons, where they carried all the mud from outside on their feet. Crowded fifty-sixty in a wagon, they'd push, whine, and curse each other, as none of them could lay down. When the guard let them out the next day, many of them walked in the daylight tired and dirty, like in a bath of mud: mud on their face, eyebrows, hands, hair, clothes... Some crouched in the wagon with their heads between their knees and didn't want to get out. The guards' clubs hit them without mercy; they would even hit dying men – sometimes they hit men that had been dead for hours...

Each night there were four-five deaths in a wagon. The corpses remained in there with the living in morbid promiscuity until someone took them away in a cart.

"We're all going to die soon... all of us here," a man told me one day when I asked him how he got there. "All of us who are part of this group have been abandoned by God. After we left Razgrad, they kept taking us places for two weeks, beating us and plundering us. We stopped during the night wherever we could, in wind or rain, even though Turkish-Bulgarian dogs robbed us and left us naked. Then we ended up here. There were around eight hundred of us... look how many of us are left... I don't know what sins we have committed, but God is evil and merciless toward us. We ended up treated like animals, we even lost our minds. Look at me, I was a peasant with a good position in my village, and now I'm scavenging for dead animals. Yesterday, I found a chicken head and I chewed it, I ate it feathers and all..."

Among the Germans sentinels, there was a group from Bavaria. Kind men like them are hard to come by. They had open hearts, and they were gentle to our people, not like the Germans who didn't allow them to rest for a second during work, but they screamed at them from morning to night:

"*Loos!... Loos!*"[50]

I befriended the Bavarians on the first day; through them, I obtained permission to sleep outside. The officer left me alone because he was afraid of them.

In the morning, they had jugs with coffee, thin and discolored – but hot. They gave me a small tart from their military satchels. It was made of two thin slices of bread with pork fat in the middle. It was good at that time, but before that, I never thought I could eat something like that.

My friends had not been in Bulgaria for long. They were working on a bridge, and they were just as hardworking as they were childish and joyful. Before coming here, they'd been on the Russian front, far in Oriental Prussia. Now, while they rested at noon, if one of them happened to fall asleep, one of their usual jokes was to shout in one's ear:

"*Hoch! Die Rüssen kommen!*"[51]

---

[50] Meaning: Keep on!

[51] Wake up! The Russians are coming!

And the one doing it laughed terribly when the other sprang up and frantically looked for his weapon, thinking he was on the battlefield near the Baltic Sea.

***

Then heavy snows started with frost and blizzards. In the wagons, where the number of people was diminishing, the blizzard was hissing through every crack, blowing fine snow inside.

On a Sunday, the officers were ordered to move everyone who was left alive to a nearby factory… to take a bath...

The guards pulled them out in the morning, screaming and hitting them with clubs, even the ones that couldn't walk.

Under the ashy purple sky, on the field covered in snow, the ghostly convoy crawled through the snow, looking more horrifying than any *Pohod na Sibir*. Whoever fell was left behind. The soldiers would kick them, pull them by their legs, and in the end, they'd leave them in the snow. People were scattered all over the field, and we knew we would find them stiff when we returned.

Whoever managed to reach the factory took their rags off in a nearly frozen room, and then got pushed from behind into a large shower room...

I saw them through the cracked door. They were shivering against the walls – skeletons with no flesh, dressed in purple skin, standing corpses, hideous bodies, all horrifying – huddling next to each other, so they wouldn't be splashed by the big sprinkler that was hanging from the ceiling.

After they finished their "bath," they looked even worse than before but just as dirty.

***

I lasted for twenty days, bravely fighting with superhuman strength against the sinister misery of this camp, against the danger that destiny, or my recklessness, had thrown me in. I failed in the end. I got sick. And I thought everything was over.

But my Bavarian friends took me to a military doctor and insisted, with all the power Germans had in those lands, to take me to a hospital.

XVII

The "Klon Evropa" hospital was set in a hotel in the center of Sofia. It started being used for prisoners after the injured Bulgarians were evacuated – and it was a true Tower of Babel. On the steps, in the hallways, and in the wide rooms of the four floors, there was a mix of buzzing in ten European languages, among which dominated the Slavonic dialects.

Together with the prisoners, several nurses called *Samaritans* lived there. They used to care for the wounded Bulgarians. Other nurses were called *Sestra*, and each was responsible for one floor.

It was a mess. In time, I learned to speak *Volapiik*, a blend of Serbian, Russian, and Bulgarian, which must have resembled the old Slavic of Cyril and Methodius, randomly dotted with Greek words, French words, and made-up phrases that I had to make up on the spot to converse with an Englishman, Turkish, or Armenian who didn't know Romanian.

At first, I was taken to the pavilion on the first floor, which was separated by a wall from the main building, where it took them a while to find a bed for me.

I was cured in three days. All I had was a light case of the flu. But the Serbian doctor, who knew what filth I was brought in from, promised to keep me there for another week to recover.

Meanwhile, I became friends with Sestra Luluşeva – a woman with a beautiful soul, originating from Greece, and who resembled a nun. With her help, I hatched a plan to remain in the hospital.

Among the sick gathered there, there was a Greek man from Kavala, called Papangellos, who was old but a passionate Venizelist. He was a pharmacist. One evening, we planned for him to declare he was a doctor of internal diseases Nobody would know otherwise. I asked through a petition written in French, addressed to Dr. Ștefanov, the chief doctor of the hospital, to let him attend a whole floor with patients, using me as a secretary and interpreter.

My request was approved. We were given the fourth floor.

As a perk of my new job, I was given a small isolated room at the end of the top floor, from where I had a wide view of the city.

***

Neither the Greek nor I knew any medicine. To adapt to the circumstances, I was borrowing books on medical subjects from a medical student named Loba-nof, which I was reading every night. I was studying all sorts of diseases, and I considered I touched all of them at least partially. I was ready to become a hypochondriac, but when I got before a patient, I'd forget everything I'd learned so far and I couldn't understand anything that was going on.

I had about ten Serbian helpers, which I gradually replaced with Romanians.

As soon as I found vacant beds, I went downstairs in the morning to receive the men brought from nearby camps. I closely inspected each of them, and I always went for the ones who seemed they were there only to skip work. Those were good for the fourth floor.

In this way, we didn't have people dying in our care on the fourth floor, and our medical competency was not questioned. Some of the actual doctors were even jealous because of this.

For diagnosis, we sneaked them all during lunch to the Serbian doctor on the first floor and wrote down everything he told me. My Greek friend wrote the prescriptions. He could do that much. Otherwise, he was useless. He was even forgetting the names of the most common illnesses, or couldn't pronounce them correctly when Ștefanov was inspecting our floor. I always had to stay behind him and whisper to him everything like we were in school – that was pointless.

"*Cacvo imă toi?*" The head doctor asked him one day, stopping before a new patient. "What's wrong with him?" I knew the man had pleurisy. Because the Greek didn't seem to remember, even though I went over the terms with him, as usual, I got behind him and whispered in French: *pleurésie*...

"*Phlegmagi*," he answered loudly and sure of his knowledge.

The Bulgarian was confused but impressed by the name of this mysterious illness, which he'd never heard of before.

That's how winter passed and I hardly felt it. In the evening, I'd walk down to the first floor to talk to the French and to a few of my friends from Bucharest – lawyers, officers, actors – who were lucky enough to have been taken in by the hospital, even though they weren't really ill. During the day, I wrote the patients' records, and read medical books or French books that I'd borrowed from Mrs. Aftalion – a Romanian woman married to someone in Sofia, admirable and brave, who was subjected to a good deal of unpleasantness from the Bulgarians in order to bring us cigarettes, books, and other necessary things for foreigners like us.

The Sestra on my floor was named Raina. She was an honest girl, with wide hips, with whom I had a strict friendship.

However, a small Samaritan from the top floor sometimes came to my room in the middle of the night, and quietly sang me a Bulgarian love song, simple like love itself. Her name was Sfetanca, and she was blonde; she wore a blue ribbon in her hair and never wore socks with her shoes.

The others got women however they could. The Bulgarians were jealous patriots and punished by banishing whomever they caught doing immoral things; the Sestras were more lenient.

To appease them, there was a woman on the second floor, older but joyful and robust, who had intimate relations with four Bulgarian soldiers at the same time. She was very happy and sang all day and worked as hard as seven men.

But women preferred the prisoners because they were usually gentle and because they had many nationalities to choose from: French, Romanian, Russian...

One morning we found a black man in the hospital yard. He was from Congo, and got trapped on the front in Thessaloniki – he was short with big lips.

His arrival made quite the impression. Every Sestra and Samaritan came to see him and surrounded him with laughter and jokes. Afraid of the crowd, he leaned against a wall in the sunlight, shivering like a black kitten. He then calmed down a bit, dared to look around him at the circle of women, and on his coal-colored face appeared a wide smile, white teeth sparkling in the sun. The Sestras got even closer. One pulled his sleeve; another touched his hair. They were joking among themselves, watching him as if he was a miracle. They had indecent curiosities, and they were touching him laughing. The women became very daring when they were together with only one man. Finally, the big retinue accompanied him to the third floor, and they went in pilgrimage at his bedside until late in the evening, to see him again and again.

The Sestras were not bad women, but they sometimes spied on each other and snitched out of jealousy.

One was especially bad about it, Cantargieva, the one in charge of the floor where the man was. She was giving everyone a hard time. With a withered face, over 40 years of age, with a straight nose and thin lips, she wore too much powder and stylish clothes. Always wearing *à jour hose* and tight varnished shoes, she walked through the yard in the afternoon or invited a friend into her room, where she would gossip about every event taking place in the hospital, including her coworkers. Everyone feared her and shivered when they saw her.

Of course, she wasn't a saint either. But nobody could catch her doing anything shameful. She was cunning and sneaky, knew everyone's sins, but knew how to conceal her own. One of her rivals whom she denounced to the hospital authority had been caught and banished. Two of the girls who had shamefully left were Navena, the dark girl who was always smiling, and the fair Paceva, a shy girl with strange colored eyes, who often had a troubled look and blushed without a reason... And others were banished in the same way.

One day Hiteva was banished, the friend of the soldier, Ivan. Because of this, there was bad blood between Cantargieva and Ivan, the leader of the hospital carriers, who was now planning to take revenge on her.

One evening, I was watching from my window as usual. Close to midnight, I saw Cantargieva in the yard. She was on duty that night. Her movements seemed weird to me. She was on guard, walking slowly, stopping, and listening around... Tiptoeing, she got near the door of the guards and looked inside through the window. Then she quickly climbed the stairs.

Ivan came behind her; he had bare feet and a bare head. He walked through the narrow yard and disappeared in the same direction as Cantargieva.

Not long after that, I heard a noise and whistling on the floor below me. A few guards came up the steps talking. I went downstairs to see what was happening.

The sick men from every room were coming out, woken up from their sleep, and they were asking what was happening in various languages.

The door to Cantargieva's room was wide open. A few Sestras were standing there, enjoying the scene. Some of the sick men were pushing from behind them to see, but the guards kept dismissing them back to their rooms.

Cantargieva was standing with her back to the window, with her arms crossed.

"Where's the black man? What did you do to him?" asked Ivan after searching every corner of the hospital.

"*Tîrsite*," she answered sharply.

So, he started searching again; under the bed, behind the curtains, above the stove, even in the stove...

"I saw him with my own eyes entering your room," he said. And he went to search the bed again. He had an idea: to lift the mattress...

Laughter then filled the room.

He found him.

The man was there, small and black, mashed between two mattresses like a raisin.

XVIII

Trivial events, long dull days, like in a prison...

I felt far away from the full and exciting life I had on Pirin-Planina!

Like a late echo of those days, one of my friends that I'd left there came to the hospital one morning. He had run away, had passed from camp to camp, reaching Sofia in the end, after many struggles.

I stayed with him, and he told me everything that had happened to them on Pirin after I left.

Stan Boldişcu left them one day. He had been called on the front. Only the Bulgarian with the supplies visited them once in a while. He called them from the valley with a long yell and left them a few hands of cornmeal or a few biscuits. And because he didn't know Romanian at all, he couldn't tell them any news of what was going on in the world, he only watched them oddly, with his small eyes like fish scales from under his bushy eyebrows. He was always in a hurry.

Abandoned there above the forests, the only ones who guarded them were the two Turkish soldiers, and our men had lost the track of days by that point, not even knowing when holidays were. Bluebells had started to bloom near the bushes; the beech trees in the valley seemed to wait for the day of St George to spring their buds. There were green butterflies on the golden dandelions, and small white flowers looking like snowflakes. Deceived by these signs of spring, people thought it was close to Easter, and they were afraid that they were going to miss it if nobody told them what date it was.

Toader Căpuzanu seemed more upset than anyone else because he was strict about having a feast on this day according to traditions.

"Brothers, what are we going to do? Easter will pass, and we won't even know it... This isn't right!"

One morning, in the early sunlight full of finch chirps, Căpuzanu came out of his shelter and said:

"Today is Palm Sunday. I saw a sign of it... Last night I dreamt I was picking catkins on the shore of the river with Father Ion. Mark my words, it's how I'm telling you – Easter is a week from today. I'll find eggs so that we can knock them like every good Christian..."

He spent a whole week getting everything ready; every evening, he'd return tired and covered in scratches, with eggs from wild birds in his cap... Spotted eggs from eagles, bigger than hen eggs, thrush eggs, magpie eggs, and shrike eggs, yellow with copper splotches, green blackbird eggs – and big ones from guinea fowls, which he said he found under roots, or in nests made of dry leaves. But he didn't have anything to use as dye. It would have been a pity to leave them plain like that for Easter, so the men boiled them in water and tree bark; from that bitter broth, they came out looking gray, the same as their souls.

On Saturday, they all got ready and checked their reflections in the stream water. From a cluster of young pines, guard Năiță brought a few green branches they used to decorate the doors to their shelters.

They all gathered around a big fire to celebrate the night of Resurrection. They watched the flames in silence with their arms around their knees, reliving memories.

"Brothers, if I am to die in this wilderness, I have but one thing to ask of you. Bury me facing the Argeș river," said Căpuzaru.

They then stood up and looked again at the village in the valley, but no light could be seen.

After a time, the fire died in the heap – and, by following the sky, it seemed to be midnight. Căpuzaru lit up a bora twig, lifted it above his head, and shouted:

"Christ has risen, brothers!"

Following his example, they all lit up the improvised candles and replied:

"Indeed, he has risen!"

While the Turks were watching them confused from the shadows, their voices echoed on the peak of the foreign mountain as they were singing:

"Christ has risen from the dead, overcoming death through death..."

***

After sunny days and cool nights through which the howling of jackals echoed from the valley, a long convoy with provisions came from Nevrocopol toward the front, on the mountain road at noon.

The men in that group were whistling to the bulls, glancing uneasily up the slope from where our men were watching them with interest.

"Which of you speaks Romanian?" asked Căpuzaru from the top of the slope.

An old Bulgarian replied:

"I know Romanian. What do you want?"

"Christ has risen!" Căpuzaru shouted to him.

The Bulgarian watched him suspiciously; he then pulled his cap over his eyes, spat at a side, and said:

"He hasn't yet! Who told you he did? He'll rise in about three weeks..."

XIX

My window had dominion over the houses around. I admired the view of hundreds of chimneys pointing to the sky for long periods of time during the summer afternoons.

It was warm and quiet. The water of the dead was shivering in the light on the red tin roofs. I used to sit there, above the city, alone for hours with a book in my lap; and through my heart, which was once full of life, passed only vague memories, images with no outline resembling the thin clouds melting in the blue sky, leaving their translucent shadow over the city as they were passing.

One time, I saw the delicate silhouette of a girl in an open window. Her chest graciously bent while holding the edge of the window with one hand, and it looked like she was watching something far away. The wide sleeve of her summer blouse slipped and revealed her arm up to her shoulder.

I couldn't see her face. Judging by her movements and her dark hair, I thought she had delicate olive skin.

I watched this apparition for a long time. Even after she went back inside, my eyes still saw her looking over the tall window sill.

In the following days, the stranger showed up again, in the same place, holding her bare arm above her head, which looked white against the shadow, like a small patch of light.

The girl couldn't see me.

But in the dullness of those afternoon hours, her sight was a fine distraction for me. As the city went to sleep drowsy from the heat, I was looking forward to seeing the window sill come alive; and when her figure showed up suddenly, I always quietly greeted her.

I couldn't see her face.
Judging by her movements and her dark hair,
I thought she had delicate olive skin

One day I felt as if she was watching a bit more persistent my way, so I waved a handkerchief. The girl quickly disappeared and returned with binoculars and watched me for a while. She then walked into the shadow of her chamber and replied to me in the same way, with her handkerchief.

That's how we acquainted ourselves. And that was the extent of our air correspondence.

She probably knew from the start that I was a prisoner of war, and being a kind woman, she wanted to give me the memory of a fleeting moment. Maybe she was as romantic and lonely as I was.

Then we started to communicate from afar by using gestures. What we were trying to say was a very simple thing actually – and we managed to share it on the third day. There are many things you can tell a person through gestures and signs! Within a few days, we went through all shades of a beginning, from a simple wave of a handkerchief, which means *bonjour*, to the unexpected gesture of blowing a kiss from afar.

I was happy with that much, what was I supposed to do? I noticed that girls were more curious in general. My friend wanted us to leave the realm of gestures, which only expressed general feelings. She soon found a new type of wireless telegraphy: she cut out big paper letters and showed them to me one by one. In turn, I ruined a bunch of printed forms from the hospital on which it was written in Slavic Cyrillic letters: *Lista za hranata*[52] or something like this – to create an alphabet.

We were too far away from one another, and the letters weren't clear. While I was trying to communicate with her in French, she replied in Bulgarian... It was impossible to understand each other in two languages that were so different. We both dropped our arms to the side in discouragement. After that, we tried to convey our messages telepathically, if we couldn't do it through gestures.

Every day, at the same time, she appeared in the light like a pastel-colored flower above the monochromatic roofs between bleak chimneys. Our thoughts

---

[52] Cooking list (Bulg.).

blended in the air. Nobody stood between us to witness it, and we didn't see anyone. I had the illusion that I was alone under the pale wide sky, in solitary silence.

Our air friendship, which was purely platonic due to the circumstances, reached a dead end and risked turning into a plain habit that kept repeating without a change.

***

On a late evening, I opened my window, and I was looking at a star from the Big Dipper, with my thoughts far away.

Black clouds were rising from toward the Balkans. A short gust of wind blew above the houses in a rush. To enjoy the nearing storm, I turned the light off and sat on the window sill, with my legs hanging out above the abyss below me.

My eyes involuntarily glanced toward the familiar window.

My Bulgarian girl was there. She had also turned her light off, and she could undoubtedly see me. A bolt of bright forked lightning revealed us at the same time.

The girl was naked...

At first, I thought it was just my imagination; but my temporarily blinded eyes still held onto the image of her white body at the window.

The next lightning showed her to me again, naked and motionless in a crude light. It was for only a moment. The night quickly wrapped up her nakedness. When the darkness was ripped apart again, the vision disappeared. All I saw was the closed window that sparkled in the light.

She had gifted all that a girl could to a war prisoner on a stormy summer night.

XX

It was the middle of winter.

The train I was on headed north, towards the Danube...

A great friend from my country, which was still an occupied territory, found out that I was in a hospital in Sofia and had intervened with the Bulgarian commandment in Bucharest, requesting for me to be brought there.

Because the train was full of soldiers, I stayed outside, on the wagon's platform, frozen to the bone. The blizzard was throwing sharp pieces of glass at my cheek. Stancio, the soldier who escorted me to Rusciuk, stood with his arms crossed over his gun and didn't speaking a word to me. His mustache was frozen.

After a while, the Bulgarian guard started looking impatient.

"We're going to pass through my village..."

"What side will it be on?"

Holding the steel vertical bar with his big brown glove that resembled a bear's paw, Stancio leaned over to show me. Then, he turned back to me in the screech of the wheels and shouted in Bulgarian:

"Tomorrow is the New Year. Would you like to stay in my village overnight?"

I knew he had married recently, and he must miss his wife terribly. However, he received orders to take me directly to my destination.

"What if we're going to get in trouble?"

Without answering, he pulled a green sheet of paper from his sleeve and looked at it. Then he folded it and put it back.

The train slowed down while going downhill.

"*Haida*!" Stancio told me.

"Are we jumping?"

"Yes."

I went down the wagon's stairs and had second thoughts.

"What are they going to say if they see us jumping?"

"They'll think you wanted to run away and I jumped after you. Come on!" he told me again, lightly pushing me from behind.

I jumped.

Behind me, Stancio rolled through the snow after he'd thrown his gun somewhere.

When we stood up, the train was departing quickly with a heavy metallic noise. In the solitude of the desolate field, the complete quiet of the winter twilight surrounded us suddenly, contrasting the uninterrupted screeching of the train that I'd heard until then.

We started walking across the field through the snow that was slowly turning to a shade of blue toward the end of a small hill from where wisps of smoke were rising in the air.

Half an hour later, we entered the village. There was still a bit of light left. Heavily-clothed women greeted us curiously and asked Stancio questions that he answered with two words every time. At the pub, old and young men were crowding to buy wine for the New Year's feast.

We turned left onto a small street.

"Are we there yet?"

"*Tucă*," replied Stancio, pushing a small gate with his shoulder. In the back-yard, I saw a small house with a low snowy roof. The light was shining through the windows.

A dog barked a few times and the door opened. At the illuminated entrance, a young woman showed up, with an old man behind her.

"Stancio!" yelled the woman with unmeasured joy.

"They'll think you wanted to run away
and I jumped after you. Come on!" he told me again,
lightly pushing me from behind

The old man still seemed healthy but had white hair and eyebrows, and he asked Stancio a lot of questions. The chubby woman helped him take his clothes off. She walked in circles around him without a word. Her eyes took him in, and she laughed with happiness.

Finally, Mister Manole turned to me:

"Romanian?"

"Yes."

"Come near the fire to warm up."

A lamp was hanging on the wall illuminating the spacious room with floors made of clay. The small windows were covered in frost. In the corner, near the door, there was a wide bed that almost reached the ceiling, built on some sort of beams that protruded from the walls, supported on the side by a rounded pole made of polished wood. You'd have to climb on a chair to get to it, and you'd have to be able to do some gymnastics. Next to the wall in the back, there was a normal bed made of wood, covered with a mat, and another bed under the window, with a striped pillow and a woolen blanket.

I sat on a chair near the stove and warmed up. Stancio put his coat, gun, and bayonet in a corner, where he also whispered something secretly to his wife. After that, Mister Manole took a big jug under his arm and went to buy wine. I gave him a few lei as well, which the old man received without a word and counted them in his palm.

Petcana, the wife, started laying out the table. With rosy cheeks, a bit sweaty, smiling eyes, chubby and sturdy, the housewife was trampling the floor under her feet. She never looked me in the eyes, and she never talked to me directly. In a big pan, she cooked an omelet made of 10 eggs with butter, in which she cut fifteen small red peppers. When the old man came back with the wine, the woman pulled out a jug of cherry brandy from a cupboard and gave us each half a cup. From the sneaky look she gave her man, I understood that she gave him more.

We sat on chairs with three legs around a small round table, in the middle of the room, each with a big slice of bread.

But the omelet was too spicy. My mouth felt like it was on fire. After two bites, I asked for water.

"He doesn't like it because he doesn't have *caciamac* (polenta)!" The woman smiled without looking me in the eye. It was a small sting directed at a Romanian, a joke the housewife threw me with envy for not liking her omelet.

We drank a glass of wine, and after that, the woman pulled a big pie out of the oven. She set it in the middle of the table. We didn't have plates or knives, so I waited to see how we were supposed to eat it. It was simple: each tore a piece with his fingers and ate it. This was the traditional New Year pie – a few thick baked sheets with onion and bacon between them.

"What is this called in Bulgarian?" I asked.

"This is called *banița*," the old man told me, wiping his mouth. "This is what we, Bulgarians, eat during feast days..."

After a few more glasses of wine, Manole stopped being bashful.

"We don't have anything against you Romanians," he suddenly remarked, turning to me. "You are all Christians like us, and in my youth, you came with the Russians to save us from slavery. Then," he said quietly, "many of our people went to Romania and returned with good sums of money... Romania is a rich country..."

He spoke to me in Bulgarian. I could understand everything, but I didn't really know how to reply.

"We have a problem with the Turks," he continued. "We are friends like cats and dogs – but before... Efendi the Turk used to come on horseback and stopped at houses day or night. The Bulgarian used to hold his horse by the reins at his gate, and the Turk went inside to visit his wife... Then he'd ask for sweet milk – but he wouldn't stand up to drink it, he commanded the Bulgarian to take it to his mouth with a spoon, as if he was a child..."

The boy was listening impassively, quietly picking up the last crumbs of *banița* from the bottom of the tray.

The meal was over.

We had plenty more to drink, and the old man was in the mood to talk. He started explaining to me a complicated political matter from the Balkans, and he mentioned *trinaisi godina* to me – about Greeks, Serbians, and about all the troubles that the "betrayal" of these cunning neighbors caused for Bulgaria...

But Stancio didn't feel like talking anymore. And Petcana didn't have patience. With shiny eyes and cheeks rosy from wine, the woman was standing up often, getting busy around the house and glancing at her man.

Finally, the man stood up with difficulty, told us "*Lecă noș*"[53] – and laid down on the bed in the back of the room to sleep.

Stancio climbed into the tall bed. Petcana cleaned off the table in the blink of an eye and signaled me to sleep on the bed near the window, where I lay dressed up, on a hard pillow.

Then the woman opened her girdle in one move, blew out the lamp, and got in bed to enjoy the night with her husband.

I couldn't fall asleep for a long time.

Turned toward the wall, I was listening to the old man's snoring and the blizzard that was howling wildly under the windows. Somewhere in the dark, an open gate or a broken shingle was moaning pitifully in the wind. I was thinking about the unexpected event that had brought me to this Bulgarian house on New Year's Eve. If I hadn't jumped off the train, I might be far now – maybe I would have arrived at my destination... But I didn't regret it. Thanks to me, two poor human beings living in times of war, were now thrown together under the same roof and were getting to enjoy some moments of humble happiness.

On the following day, we woke up before daylight and started walking toward the nearest train station, to catch the train.

---

[53] Good night (Bulg.).

XXI

I reached Rusciuk at ten at night.

I waited in a room of the guards' building, with a Bulgarian officer and sleepy soldiers, with a sour smell of tobacco, until a high-graded soldier came looking for me, searched me, and seized all the papers and letters I had in my pockets.

I was lucky: a Bulgarian courier was leaving the same night for Bucharest. Accompanied by him, I reached the Danube's shores within the hour.

In the dark night, I finally spotted the river from where I was taken so long ago; with a racing heart, I listened to the waves flowing – and recognized the river's voice...

I didn't know if it was luck or my own doing, but I had escaped everything...

I couldn't see anything on the other side because it was dark, and there were no stars. Far away downstream, I could see a few small lights glittering...

And I could hear the dogs barking at Giurgiu.

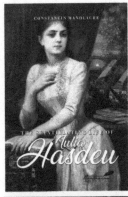

Check out these and other great titles at
CenterforRomanianStudies.com